DATE DUE

PSYCHOLOGY AND THE
TEACHING CHURCH

PSYCHOLOGY
AND THE
TEACHING CHURCH

Jesse H. Ziegler

ABINGDON PRESS
new york 🅐 nashville

PSYCHOLOGY AND THE TEACHING CHURCH

Copyright © 1962 by Abingdon Press

Library of Congress Catalog Card Number: 62-16813

SET UP, PRINTED, AND BOUND BY THE
PARTHENON PRESS, AT NASHVILLE,
TENNESSEE, UNITED STATES OF AMERICA

to my Mother and Father

whose devout Christian lives and
practical psychology have greatly influenced
what I am and know

To my Mother and Father

PREFACE

No one of us is disposed to argue against the idea that the first qualification of a Christian teacher is that he shall be a good man, but many of us are prepared to follow that immediately by saying that he must also be a person with much knowledge. It is to share significant knowledge that books are written and published and to satisfy the hunger for more knowledge that they are read. But not all knowledge is of equal importance to the teacher of people who participates in a ministry of the church.

Two major areas of knowledge are important for the Christian teacher. First, he must know God personally and intimately. He must know God firsthand rather than only from what others say about him. He must know him as he may be known through the Bible in which he has spoken a word for every man. He must know him through the history and tradition of the church. He must know him through personal experience. This knowledge of and thought about God is the content of theology defined in its strictest sense.

The Christian teacher must also know man. God makes all his resources available for the redeeming of men. The gospel is good news to be broadcast, but the nature of the hearer must be taken into account if the good news is to be heard. How does a person come to be what he is? Why do certain ideas emerge and come to be present in people? How do persons differ as a function of age? How can people be helped to work together for desired ends? How can a person be changed from neurosis to health? Such questions are illustrative of those to which answers about man are needed by the person who is called to be a teacher in the church.

Knowledge about persons comes from a variety of sources. It should be emphasized that there is a kind of knowledge about man and understanding of his nature which comes through the witness of those who wrote the Scriptures. Among us such phrases as "created in the image of God," "little lower than God," "all have sinned," "all we like sheep have gone astray," suggest something of the nature of man as he is seen by writers of the Scriptures. God's most profound word not only about himself, but about man as he was meant to be, is found in Jesus Christ.

Some understanding of persons is also to be seen in the creations of novelists, dramatists, painters, and sculptors. Falkner, Dostoevski, Camus, Kafka, Williams, Picasso, and Rouault give portraits of man that may not be very pleasant to our refined taste, but to see persons as these artists help us to see them is to come closer to understanding some aspects of man that most of us are inclined ordinarily to overlook.

8

A third way to come to knowledge about man is by way of the kind of empirical and systematic study that is characteristic of contemporary psychology. It is on this approach that we are concentrating in this little book. No claim is made that this is the only or even the best way to come to an understanding of man. It must be said that here is another approach to an understanding of man which cannot safely be ignored if we are to be well prepared for our task.

I can lay no claim to speak in representative fashion for the discipline of psychology. The material which is presented is a portion of what I have found most helpful in my years of work to contribute to firm foundations for the church's work of Christian education.

Nor can any claim be made for any profoundly original contribution. To attempt to acknowledge my full indebtedness could only result in failure. The idea of the book began in a course in psychological foundations for Christian education offered in Garrett Biblical Institute and elaborated in years of teaching in Bethany Biblical Seminary. For the give and take with my students I am deeply grateful.

Chapter I was developed through stages of presentation as a paper to the Professors and Research Section of the Division of Christian Education of the National Council of Churches and to the North Carolina Pastors' Convention at the Divinity School of Duke University. Chapter IV was presented to and discussed in developing forms with the Editors' Section of the Division of

Christian Education of the National Council of Churches and to the Curriculum Study Conference of the Church of the Brethren. Major parts of Chapter V were presented to the faculty of Union Theological Seminary (Richmond) and to the seven regional meetings of professors of Christian education in the theological schools of the United States and Canada. To all the people who were kind enough to respond in these various settings I am grateful.

Most of all I am grateful for the challenge of putting all the material except Chapter III in manuscript form for delivery at the Fourth Annual Willson Lectures at the Methodist Training School at Mount Sequoiah, Arkansas, and for the encouragement given by so many requests for publication.

My warmest thanks are extended to my colleague Dr. Charles L. Taylor, Jr. for his reading of the greater part of the manuscript and his helpful suggestions and to Mrs. Robert Thompson and Mrs. Carl Bookwalter who worked conscientiously at translating my script into accurate and readable typescript.

JESSE H. ZIEGLER

CONTENTS

11

I

Foundations for Christian Education in Contemporary Personality Theory

PERSONALITY THEORY IN THE FIELD OF PSYCHOLOGY

The history of contemporary psychology is encompassed within the last three quarters of a century. During that time two main streams of psychology have been developing side by side. The experimental psychologists, with their roots in the work of Ebbinghaus, Wundt, Helmholtz, Titchener, and Külpe, represent one stream with its methods more closely related to the natural scientists. The personality psychologists, with their roots in the work of Freud, Jung, and McDougall, were much more closely related to the field of medicine.

While personality theory has developed side by side with general psychology it has never felt bound to the rigorous methods nor the proper problems of the other. Furthermore, it has been primarily functional in its orientation, reflecting its origins in the clinic and in psychotherapy. It has never wanted to pursue problems just because they were problems but only in order to be of help to people who were in difficulty. Personality theory has been deeply concerned about motivational

13

processes, while general psychology in its beginnings paid little attention to motivation. Personality theorists have by definition and by interest been chiefly concerned with the study of the person as a whole rather than with very limited aspects of the functioning of the person. Because the personality theorist is willing to accept from any quarter data that deals with the behavior of man he serves a very useful integrative function in the field of psychology.

If we were to attempt to define specifically what is meant by personality we would be supplied with a different definition by each theorist. It seems most satisfactory to say with Calvin Springer Hall and Gardner Lindzey, "Personality consists concretely of a set of values or descriptive terms which are used to describe the individual being studied according to the variables or dimensions which occupy a central position within the particular theory utilized." [1]

We should be clear as to what the psychologist is doing when he is at work as a theory builder. Theories are built in order to provide a framework of meaningful relationships into which the empirical data regarding man may be fitted. Such a framework is necessary because it is only as the empirical data is seen in its contextual framework that it is possible to discover what additional investigations need to be made to complete the picture. Furthermore, it is the theory, when concisely stated, that

[1] Theories of Personality (New York: John Wiley & Sons, Inc., 1957), p. 9.

begins to make possible the prediction of behavior. Discrete and unrelated data can never make prediction possible. It is the theory that takes due account of and is built out of the data that provides bases for prediction. It may be said then that the theory builder engages in his function so that we may see where further work needs to be done and how the work that has been done may be useful in prediction.

To take the responsibility for speaking of foundations in personality theory is to speak of a very diverse field. For the most part theory builders accept the same set of facts or data. But they look at the data from different perspectives and arrange the data in different ways. For this reason there are twelve relatively different types of personality theory in the study by Lindzey and Hall. The international survey edited by Henry Philip David and Helmut von Bracken covers an even wider range.[2]

APPROACH

When confronted with an opportunity to deal with personality theory a psychologist is always faced with a dilemma. Shall he choose his own one or two favorite approaches to personality theory and develop those at some length in the hope that others may find them equally valuable? Or shall he give a brief descriptive summary and critique of some ten or twelve best known theories? Each of these has its own peculiar value. For

[2] *Perspectives in Personality Theory* (New York: Basic Books, Inc., 1957).

this work it seemed most useful to select from contemporary personality theory seven trends and examine these for their significance for Christian education.

It is not practical in the light of the limitations of this work to refer to the research studies that are basic to each of the trends. For a more careful examination of the trends themselves one of the most helpful summaries is the volume by Hall and Lindzey to which reference has already been made. Reference may be found there and also in some notes within this presentation to original sources the interested student may wish to consult.

The questions to be dealt with in this chapter are (1) What clear and rather widely accepted trends may be seen in contemporary personality theory, and (2) What is the significance of such theoretical assumptions for Christian education?

TRENDS SIGNIFICANT FOR CHRISTIAN EDUCATION

A. *Personality can be best understood only when looked at in depth*

Although in philosophy there had been hints of an awareness of a level of personality that was not readily open to conscious scrutiny, the early experimentalists gave no indication that such parts of the personality, if they existed in reality, were of any interest to the psychologist. It was in the medical psychology of Sigmund Freud that the first hints appeared within psychology of the importance of looking at persons in depth if their motivations are to be understood and, indeed, if their normal

16

behavior is to be understood. Jung, Horney, and Murray are also strong supporters of the view that unconscious motivations play a major role in human behavior. Many other personality theorists give a more limited emphasis to this view.

The essence of this trend in personality theory is that much of the behavior of persons can be understood only as one postulates the existence of levels of the mind that are not easily available to conscious scrutiny. The mind is like an iceberg, only a small part of which may be observed directly; and the theorists who lean heavily in this direction would draw further comparison with the iceberg. Actually it is the great mass of the ice which is concealed which largely determines the behavior of the mass. Or to take another figure of speech, the mind is like the composition of the earth. The formation of even that part of the earth which one can readily see can never be understood by looking only at the surface. The earthquakes in Chile, the volcanoes in Hawaii, the slanting and upthrust rock formations in the Sierra Nevada mountains, can be understood best within the theory that there is a part of the world which is dynamic and in which there is great energy of which little can be seen on the surface.

The depth psychologists, as they are sometimes called, propose that the seat and source of much of the energy of the person is in a part of the mind which must be thought of as unconscious, since its activity is not readily available for observation. Within this unconscious are the primitive and largely biological drives of the organism. Here too is the repository of experiences that are heavily charged emotionally and that have been repressed or purposefully forgotten, and here are also some taboos and prohibitions of the culture of which the person is a part and which have been incorporated in the self.

There is a constant dynamic condition within this unconscious. Various defense mechanisms are employed to prevent objectionable impulses from appearing in the conscious mind or in overt behavior. The drives and conflicts within the unconscious exercise a profound influence upon the overt behavior of the person as well as upon his conscious thought processes. They constantly oppose themselves to any exercise of pure rationality. Rationalization is the covert assignment of acceptable motives to unacceptable behavior rather than the use of reason by the conscious mind.

While there is not the kind of rigorous scientific validation for the material which is used in support of these theoretical positions which may be found in some of the work of the experimentalists, yet there is here the kind of vivid description and imagery that speaks more adequately to the condition of man who finds himself forced to say, "I do not understand my own actions. For I do not do what I want, but I do the very thing I hate." (Rom. 7:15 R.S.V.)

What are the implications for Christian education of such a theoretical position? First, since one of the major ways in which character is formed is by unconscious identification with important adult figures in the life of the growing person, much more careful scrutiny must be given to the quality of leadership figures which are provided for growing persons. This is meant to emphasize the strength of unconscious influence completely apart from all words and experiences only as a result of what and who the teacher or leader is.

Second, since it is the parents who are of so much influence in the determination of what the unconscious motivations of the child will be, a much heavier emphasis in our educational approaches to the parents is indicated. This will be spoken of in another context.

Third, much more sophistication is required regarding the limits of what can be done in the training of a person in making voluntary choices and judgments. Certainly we must not underestimate the rational and deliberate activities of the mind, but our real danger is that they are overemphasized.

Fourth, we may need to see one of the valid and important tasks of Christian education as the provision of each individual with some basic understanding of the defense mechanisms by means of which the unconscious part of him so profoundly affects the development of character. This may not seem to be suitable material to teach in the church, but if the development of the mature Christian who understands his own motivations is the goal, then such specific purposes are entirely appropriate.

B. *Persons can be understood only when perceived as wholes*

From Paul's anthropology, from Descartes' philosophy, and from Wundt's atomistic psychology man has suffered from being only partially understood because of the tendency to study isolated parts or functions. A notable attempt to remove this roadblock to a better understanding of personality is to be found in the holistic or organismic approach. This may be seen in the psychobiology of Adolph Meyer, the psychosomatics of Dunbar or Weiss, and the psychology and neurology of Goldstein. Jung, Sullivan, Allport, Murray, Sheldon, Angyal, Rogers, and Murphy all lay strong emphasis in their personality theory on the organismic point of view. Let us examine the main tenets of such an approach to personality theory.

Certain characteristics are to be seen throughout organismic theory although not all are to be seen in all theorists who give general support. This approach starts with the organism as a whole and insists that no part nor function can ever be understood when studied apart from the organism. It emphasizes unity, consistency, and integration as representative of the normal organism. This unity and integration may be disturbed by overwhelming threats from within or without. This approach to personality theory generally assumes one sovereign drive, such as self-realization, rather than a multiplicity of drives. It does not deny the effect of environment but tends to stress the inherent possibilities of the organism for development and change. It holds that more is to be learned from study of the single individual totally than from the study of one part or function in many persons.

There are many rather obvious supporting indications of the soundness of this trend in personality theory. Medicine knows quite well that some things can best be learned from the study of a heart separated from the body in which it functions, but the living function of the heart can never be understood in this way because it is affected by the functioning of the adrenal glands and the sympathetic nervous system. In the psychology of a person it is completely impossible to understand the drive to eat on the basis of relative emptiness of the stomach apart from the relief of anxiety which is accomplished by taking in food. It is impossible to understand the sexual drive on the basis of rhythms of the body apart from the whole experience of the person with expressions of affection during his entire life up to that moment. Even memory cannot be understood solely in terms of repetition or vividness of the impression apart from the need of the organism in its own defense either to remember or forget an experience.

What are the implications of holistic theory for Christian education? First, is it not necessary to concede that it is unrealistic to speak of spiritual development as though it is separate and apart from the education of the person as a whole? The other side of this coin is a much more serious consideration of the idea that a person is not educated as a person without taking into account the spiritual dimension—but we shall discuss this later.

21

Second, everything that affects the student will affect his learning of religion. The functioning of his endocrines, his experience of love and security in his home, his acceptance or rejection by his peers—these and all other parts of his total experience as an organism will affect his learning of religion. Third, it is the total person of the teacher which will influence the student. We have here simply another re-enforcement of the first implication in the preceding section. Words alone do not suffice; it requires the total person.

C. *Personality can be understood best when seen as rooted in culture*

Freud, although in a very real sense the father of contemporary personality theorizing, saw personality as rooted chiefly in a kind of biological instinctivism. Building on the profound insights of this great and seminal thinker and partially in reaction to a too great emphasis on the biological factors, the work of Adler, Fromm, Horney, and Sullivan demonstrates the profound manner in which personality finds its roots in society. For them the psychology of personality becomes a social psychology with warm and cordial relations with sociology and anthropology. All of these workers emphasize the influence of social factors in shaping personality.

Fromm gives attention to the way in which a particular society molds its members so that they carry and preserve its values. Horney stresses the intimate factors in the life of the family which give form to the personality. Sullivan is most interested in the interpersonal relations within the family and especially with the manner in which the mothering person contributes to the structure of the emerging personality. Adler seeks throughout society for influences which contribute to the motivation of the individual. All of these approaches would hold that the individual and society are interdependent; that not only does the individual have his roots in the culture, but also that the culture is shaped by individuals and is subject to the efforts of individuals to change the form of the culture.

These trends toward emphasizing the social roots of personality have serious implications for Christian education. First, this approach suggests that in the study of the Scriptures the people who are written about must always be seen standing within a cultural context which helped to make them and their ideas what they were. Second, there is again the suggestion that in Christian education much more attention must be given to the education of the culture carriers—that is, to the parents. It is in the relation of child to parent that the child encounters in primary form the expectations and the prohibitions of the society in which he will live.

Third, Christian education will be wise to see that, since it is the culture through its various institutions which forms personality, an adequate strategy will make use of these agencies and work through them in influencing the growing person. Schools, Scouts, and clubs all become channels through which the church will reach out through culture to the developing person. Fourth, Christian education will work at the preparation of persons to be in the best sense "reformers" of culture. It will see that in the reformation or transformation of culture individuals of the next generation will be reached most profoundly.

D. *"Psychological environment" is of utmost importance in personality theory*

An increasing number of personality theorists are coming to realize that it is not sufficient to see the nature of the physical and social environment within which the person stands in order to understand the person. It is more important to see that environment *as it is seen by the person who experiences it.* This point is made vigorously by Freud, Sullivan, Murray, Angyal, Goldstein, and Rogers; but perhaps the person who has made the point most vividly is Kurt Lewin. In his topological psychology he uses geometrical figures to represent relationships in such a way that they may be handled mathematically.

Let us see this issue as it is put by Lewin. Lewin would

Figure 1

say that the only legitimate field of study for the psychologist interested in personality is the "life space." By the life space he means all that is related to a person who is enclosed in a physical and social environment.

Proceeding from the general to the specific Lewin would differentiate within the life space a person who is related to the physical and social environment and yet separated from it by his own psychological environment. The relation of the person to the physical and social environment he would represent thus:

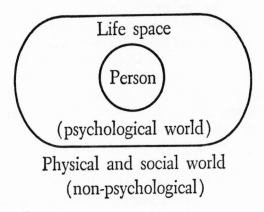

Physical and social world
(non-psychological)

Figure 2

It may be objected that this is just playing with mathematical pictures and indeed some of Lewin's critics have said this of him. There is, however, a profound truth represented in these symbols that can be ignored only at

the cost of failing to understand much of human behavior. Let us put this very simply.

Eight-year-old Stanley is swung by his father into four
feet of water in a swimming pool. He sees the water as
soft, supporting, and as something that provides pleasure.
He jumps, swims, dives, splashes, and thoroughly enjoys
the water. On the opposite side of the pool in the same
depth of water Johnny's father attempts to persuade
Johnny to jump into the water. The more he urges the
more Johnny pulls back, whimpers, and exhibits signs of
fear. He sees the water as threatening, engulfing, blind-
ing, choking, and in every way something to be avoided.
It is precisely the same pool; the boys are the same age,
but they see the swimming pool quite differently and
have quite different feelings about it. Putting it in another way, the psychological environment which separates them from and relates them to their physical
environment is quite different. Similar examples could
be taken from many fields.

In learning psychology, in social psychology, and in
psychopathology it has become increasingly clear that
differing perceptions of and feelings about identical physical and social environments must be taken into account
for any adequate understanding of behavior.

Some implications of this idea for Christian education
are immediately apparent. First, the question of greatest
importance to the curriculum writer or designer is, "How
does the student for whom the curriculum is designed
see this problem, this story, or this scene from a drama?"

It cannot be assumed that the same problem, story, or scene will mean to ten-year-olds what it does to the teacher or the curriculum writer. Indeed it requires the greatest sensitivity to have any certainty that an adult is providing various materials that will say to the child what the teacher wants to say. This is precisely the point in much of the controversy over demythologizing the New Testament.

Second, the teacher must try hard to anticipate how the learner will perceive what he is trying to do. A teacher may be quite sincere in his stern demand for a degree of order in a church-school class and may expect everyone to see him as fair-minded, but Johnny, who already felt abused when he arrived at church school, sees the demands of the teacher as evidence that even his church-school teacher simply does not understand boys.

Third, it may be necessary to go so far as to say, "It is not what God or the Church really is that will be determinative in the life of the learner, but what he sees God or the Church to be." This may be seen as radical, but from the psychologist's view it is true. Christian doctrine holds that God is the unchanging one, and yet in the providence of God it seems necessary for him to become incarnate in Jesus Christ so that men may get a clear perception of his unfailing and pursuing love. The provision of a clear perception of God seems to have been important even in his providence.

We are not meaning to suggest that the objective world is not important. It is to be hoped that there is close cor-

27

respondence between the objective and subjective, but it is the subjective or psychological world that largely determines the functioning of the individual.

E. The perceived self occupies an important position in personality theory

Throughout the history of man's thought about himself there has been an effort to discover within man some agent which organizes, guides the development of, or shapes the character of the person. For the longest period of time this function was given to the soul, but the idea of soul as such has largely been rejected in contemporary psychological theory. It is strange, however, that with the rejection of the idea of soul there is appearing the concept of the self as a differentiated portion of the perceived or phenomenal world of the individual.

Many theorists make place for the self concept. It is prominent in the theories of Adler, Horney, Sullivan, Allport, Cattell, Angyal, Goldstein, and Rogers. Probably most attention has been given to the concept in the work of Carl Rogers who places such importance on this concept that the rationale of his whole approach to psychotherapy is built upon a simple idea, viz., the best vantage point from which to view the personality is from where the individual who is reporting stands.

In Rogers' theory (1) the self develops from the interaction of the organism with the environment, (2) it introjects the values of other people and perceives them in a distorted manner, (3) it is constantly striving for internal consistency, (4) the organism behaves in ways that are consistent with the concept of the self, (5) experiences not consistent with the self are seen as threats, (6) the self changes with maturation and learning.[3] Some of the early work of Prescott Lecky shows the relation of the self concept to learning but this will be discussed in a later chapter.

If one accepts the basic tenets of this trend within personality theory some implications for Christian education are suggested. First, the most efficient approach to education can be made only if the teacher has a rather clear idea about the nature of the learner's perception of himself. Does he see himself as unable, uninterested, or unwilling to learn in this field? Does he see himself as liked by the teacher and as valued by the class? These and other perceptions will profoundly influence his learning.

Second, the teacher who is aware of this trend will ask himself very seriously what he wants to contribute to the learner's self concept. Does he want most to help him to see himself as "created in the image of God"? Does he want to emphasize the concept of "being totally depraved"? These questions must be clearly faced since persons are inclined to behave, according to this theory, in a manner consistent with their perception of self.

Third, the educator does well to ask himself what concept of the self held by the learner his method of teaching assumes. Does it assume a concept of the self as a

[3] Hall and Lindzey, *op. cit.*, p. 478.

29

kind of sponge whose chief characteristic is its ability to soak up material in which it is immersed and release it when squeezed? Does it assume a concept of the self as a participant in the processes of learning? Again it is good to remind ourselves that the organism is likely to behave in the manner which is consistent with the concept of the self and this concept arises in response at least partly to the concepts of the self held by significant people in the environment.

F. Being and nonbeing as modes of understanding is a new and inviting trend

It is scarcely fair to claim that in personality theory there is a well-established trend toward using the concepts of being and nonbeing as modes of understanding. Yet the possibility of stimulating further reading on the effect that existentialism is having upon contemporary European psychology and psychiatry and to a lesser extent on the American scene is irresistible. Since only brief reference can be made to this trend dependence must be placed on your reading such recent works as those by Rollo May, Viktor Frankl, and others.[4] Although Frankl has done much to stimulate thought through his writing, this section is more deeply indebted to May.

Personality theory after this mode is based on the idea that "the grasping of the being of the other person oc-

[4] May, et al. (eds.), *Existence* (New York: Basic Books, Inc., 1958); Frankl, *The Doctor and the Soul* (New York: Alfred A. Knopf, Inc., 1955).

curs on a quite different level from our knowledge of specific things about him. . . . The data forms itself into a configuration given in the encounter with the person himself. . . . We can at least say that knowing another human being, like loving him, involves a kind of union, a dialectical participation with the other." "The encounter . . . may potentially be very anxiety-arousing. It may also be joy-creating." "The therapist [teacher] understandably may be tempted for his own comfort to abstract himself from the encounter. . . ." [5]

Some of the most important tenets in existentialist analytic theory are: (1) Central is the realization of being and the corollary acceptance of nonbeing (in death, anxiety, hostility). (2) Anxiety is the experience of the threat of imminent nonbeing. Anxiety is seen as having an ontological base, which distinguishes it from fear. (3) The person is a being-in-the-world, but a major problem is that people have lost their world, have become estranged from people, nature, and their own bodies. This results from conceiving of the world only in symbol and abstraction. This way of conceiving of the world, although important and proper for precise thought, leaves the person feeling estranged and alone.

The implications of this approach to personality theory seem to be of considerable importance for Christian education. First, there is the suggestion that in true education there is a kind of personality sharing which is seen much too rarely. The relationship between teacher and

[5] May, op. cit., p. 38.

student is meaningless unless there is encounter or communion in which true knowledge of another person comes about.

Second, there is the suggestion that, at least in Christian teaching, we look more honestly and realistically at the possibility and perhaps even the imminence of nonbeing. If even in anxiety we may see the threat of imminent nonbeing then it seems tragic if the good news that death and hate are vanquished in Christ is not shared. It can never be realistically shared, however, unless we are honest about the possibility of nonbeing in death, hate, and destruction.

Third, it is clearly suggested that we have a responsibility for helping persons to rediscover their world— *"the structure of meaningful relationships within which a person exists and in the design of which he participates."* [6] It is quite possible that some forms of Christian teaching may have helped to alienate man from his own body, from love, from his world. Should not Christian teaching now assist in the restoration of the relationships which will help to give life meaning?

Fourth, Christian teaching may help to break the slavery of time as measured by clock and calendar and restore the function of time as a means whereby man sees his own experience in light of the distant past and the conception of a distant future. Existence is not measured by a day or a year but as seen by God, in whose

[6] *Ibid.,* p. 59.

eyes a thousand years are as a day and a day as a thousand years.

G. Data regarding direct God-man encounter is still ignored

Critics of the written history of the American scene have pointed out that history cannot be written accurately when it is written as though there is no God. The same kind of statement can be made regarding personality theory. For anyone to whom the phenomena which are depicted so vividly in the Scriptures are also the data of contemporary experience of men with God, the writing of personality theory as if God is not a major fact is incomprehensible.

It is only in the last fifteen or twenty years that there is again evident a genuine interest in trying to see the God-man encounter as a relevant datum in the building of personality theory. Even at that the only efforts being made are by psychologists working within the setting of theological education. Johnson, Oates, and I have addressed ourselves to this problem. Johnson has attempted an integrated theory of personality in which he makes room for the I-Thou encounter with God, along with the I-Me encounter with the self, the I-It encounter with the world of things, and the I-We encounter with other people.[7] Oates deals with the God-man encounter as at

[7] Paul E. Johnson, *Personality and Religion* (Nashville: Abingdon Press, 1957), Chapter 13.

the very heart of the personality. He has done significant and painstaking work on this matter.[8] I have attempted to set the development of the Spirit as resultant of the God-man encounter in the overall framework of psychoanalytic personality structure.[9]

The efforts to date in this area leave much to be desired and little has been done to project empirical studies that might be suggested by the work of these and other interested scholars.

Even with what has been accomplished thus far there are certain suggestions that present themselves for Christian educators. First, the Christian teacher will try to help his learners to see the truth within the stories of God-man encounter which are told in such vivid terms in the Bible. Second, he will try to help his learners to know that the truth received from any such encounter claimed by a person must be tested against truth which derives from the Bible, the Church, and other trusted sources. Third, he will keep in mind that he can never control where God will be. Indeed he cannot even claim any complete knowledge of God simply because God is God. Fourth, after coming to know God as well as he permits one to know him the teacher will try to make provision that his students will walk where God is likely

[8] Wayne E. Oates, *Religious Dimensions of Personality* (New York: Association Press, 1957).

[9] Marvin J. Taylor (ed.), *Religious Education* (Nashville: Abingdon Press, 1960), Chapter 3.

Lawrence C. Little (ed.), *Christian Adult Education* (Pittsburgh: University of Pittsburgh Press, 1959), Chapter 15.

to be so that they too may experience the great and decisive encounter.

No claim is made that these trends in personality theory are not debatable. Each of them commands a considerable following in contemporary psychology, and it is for that reason that it seems wise to give heed to the suggestions for our field that come from them.

II

Foundations for Christian Education in Learning Theory

As we turn to the field of learning theory it should be clear that we are moving into a much more restricted area of psychological study and theory than the discussion of contemporary personality theory. Some psychologists hold quite firmly that it is only as we come to an understanding of learning that we lay any basis for global understanding of the person. In any case, as Christian educators we should want to have whatever insight may come from the best thinking in this field.

Just when we think we understand the learning process an unexpected event occurs that makes us re-examine what we know. We may be somewhat like the farmer in Hobart Mowrer's story who was trying to teach a parrot to talk. He stood in front of the bird and said "Say 'Uncle'." The bird persisted in maintaining silence. Finally he became exasperated and began hitting the parrot on the head with a stick when it would not talk. Still the bird remained silent. In utter disgust, he picked the parrot up and threw it out into the chicken house. He had scarcely gotten back in the house before he heard a great commotion among the chickens. When he went out there was the parrot standing in front of a chicken hitting it on the head with a stick and saying in raucous voice, "Say 'Uncle'. Say 'Uncle'." [1]

It seems safe to make several assumptions regarding those who read this chapter. First, it is probably safe to assume that each of us has had some exposure to a course in educational psychology or learning theory in which we were introduced to Thorndyke, Hull, Pavlov, Guthrie, Skinner, Kohler, or Tolman. If it has been in recent years we may have become acquainted with Spence, Miller, Mowrer, Rotter, and Hebb. Second, it may be safe to assume that as educators of people we find ourselves not entirely satisfied with the contribution that these investigators have made to our own competence. We may remain unconvinced that all the work with rats and dogs and chimpanzees has very much significance for our work as teachers. It is hoped that we have no serious question about the ultimate value of these inquiries and only that we want help in doing better our own tasks.

Several possible courses of action seem open in this presentation. One course might be to give critical examination in brief form to each of the classical theories of learning with their more recent deviations. Another course would be to take a more attractive theory such as re-enforcement theory or insight theory, explicate it thoroughly, and try to discover the implications for the

[1] O. H. Mowrer, *Learning Theory and Personality Dynamics* (New York: The Ronald Press, 1950), p. 573.

work in which we are engaged. Still another might be to take three or four dynamic factors that are quite influential in learning, that are relevant to us in our work, and come to some clearer understanding of the way in which they effect learning.

In the light of our limitations and purposes, it is the latter course that has been chosen. First I shall quote from Ernest R. Hilgard, whose summary of learning theory probably remains the best, regarding the practical applications of learning theory for the person who is involved in education.[2] Then we shall look in some greater detail at four factors that play a dynamic role in learning in the belief that more careful attention to these factors will contribute to the improvement of Christian education. The factors which will be examined are taken from quite different psychological viewpoints and in themselves are quite catholic.

PRACTICAL IMPLICATIONS OF LEARNING THEORY

It is not certain that all learning theorists would agree on the following matters but it is reasonable to assume that a large proportion would. These matters of agreement will serve to provide some guidance to all those who are engaged in the educational process.

1. In deciding who should learn what, the capacities of the learner are very important. Brighter people can learn things less bright ones cannot learn; in general, older children can

[2] Theories of Learning (New York: Appleton-Century-Crofts, Inc., 1956).

learn more readily than younger ones; the decline of ability with age, in the adult years, depends upon what it is that is being learned.

2. A motivated learner acquires what he learns more readily than one who is not motivated. . . .

3. Motivation that is too intense (especially pain, fear, anxiety) may be accompanied by distracting emotional states, so that excessive motivation may be less effective than moderate motivation for learning some kinds of tasks, especially those involving difficult discriminations.

4. Learning under the control of reward is usually preferable to learning under the control of punishment. Correspondingly, learning motivated by success is preferable to learning motivated by failure. . . .

5. Learning under intrinsic motivation is preferable to learning under extrinsic motivation.

6. Tolerance for failure is best taught through providing a backlog of success that compensates for experienced failure.

7. Individuals need practice in setting realistic goals for themselves, goals neither so low as to elicit little effort nor so high as to foreordain to failure. Realistic goal-setting leads to more satisfactory improvement than unrealistic goal-setting.

8. The personal history of the individual, for example, his reaction to authority, may hamper or enhance his ability to learn from a given teacher.

9. Active participation by a learner is preferable to passive reception when learning, for example, from a lecture or a motion picture.

10. Meaningful materials and meaningful tasks are learned more readily than nonsense materials and more readily than tasks not understood by the learner.

11. There is no substitute for repetitive practice in the overlearning of skills (for instance, the performance of a concert pianist), or in the memorization of unrelated facts that have to be automatized.

12. Information about the nature of a good performance, knowledge of his own mistakes, and knowledge of successful results, aid learning.

13. Transfer to new tasks will be better if, in learning, the learner can discover relationships for himself, and if he has experience during learning of applying the principles within a variety of tasks.

14. Spaced or distributed recalls are advantageous in fixing material that is to be long retained.[3]

The psychologist can scarcely say today that there is a well-defined set of "laws of learning." The foregoing summary from Hilgard comes about as close as it may be possible to come to such a set of laws. For further elaboration of any of these or for supporting data the reader is referred to Hilgard or the source materials to which he makes reference.

DYNAMIC FACTORS IN THE LEARNING PROCESS

A. *Sublimation*

Although sublimation is usually listed among the defense mechanisms of the personality, it is not customarily listed in the factors which influence the learning process. Yet educators who are psychoanalytically oriented or

[3] From: *Theories of Learning*, Second Edition, by Ernest R. Hilgard. Copyright © 1956, Appleton-Century-Crofts, Inc. Reprinted by permission of the publisher Appleton-Century-Crofts. Pp. 486-87.

those therapists who are dealing with educational problems are quite aware of the major role played by sublimation in making learning possible. Let us look briefly at the meaning of sublimation and its relation to learning.

In discussing sexual sublimations Freud said, "The most important vicissitude which an instinct can undergo seems to be sublimation; here both object and aim are changed, so that what was originally a sexual instinct finds satisfaction in some achievement which is no longer sexual but has a higher social or ethical valuation." [4] Henry Murray said, "*Sublimation* . . . should be applied to a form of substitution in which a primitive act or cathection is replaced by an act or cathection that is less crude and less objectionable." [5] Some writers object to using the criterion of social valuation in defining sublimation. This objection does not seem to me to be well founded for it is precisely the fact that the more primitive form of behavior is acceptable neither to the parental figures nor to the embryonic internalized regulatory structures that makes the deflection of aim necessary and possible. It is the social approval of behavior in which there has been a substitution of aim or object that makes sublimation a desirable developmental defense against anxiety.

The kind of learning that must take place as a child starts to school requires the investment of great amounts

[4] *Collected Papers* (London: Hobart Press, 1950), V, 132-33.

[5] *Explorations in Personality* (New York: Oxford University Press, 1938), p. 394.

of psychic energy. Sublimation is important as a dynamic factor in learning because it is through sublimation of the primitive sexual drives of the preschooler that this libido or psychic energy is made available for investment in the learning process. If this libido is finding unde-flected or outright expression toward its original goal it is not available for the looking and curiosity which are such necessary parts of the child who is able to learn readily in school.

One therapist tells of a little girl who went to one school after another, never able to stay in one more than three days, and who was willing only to lie down and play in masturbatory fashion. Another tells of the first-grade boy who was brought to school every morning and met every noon by his very seductive mother. This boy could give no attention to learning to read but seemed to spend his time waiting to see his mother again. He was an only child, and the father and mother were separated. In these cases no learning could take place within the school situation because there was no sublimation of the libidinal drives.

Similar situations are seen repeatedly in high-school or college students who are tremendously involved in strong id drives with regard to sexual expression. No creative academic work is possible unless these drives are some-how partially deflected with some of their energy being made available for study and creative work. Some writers hold that no genital drives can be sublimated. It would seem to me that there is plenty of evidence that it is only as genital drives are sublimated at least partially that you get creative work in teen-agers or adults.

In our culture formal education begins just at the time when, according to Freud, the child is entering upon a period of latency of sexual urges. This has real significance and meaning since if these urges are now being partially repressed and partially sublimated there should be much psychic energy available for learning, and that such is the case may be readily observed in the huge investment of energy in learning during these years.

B. Identification

Let us now consider identification as a second factor in the learning process. We have long known that children learn some behavior by watching someone else and then repeating the act in somewhat similar manner. This has been called imitation. It might be called social learning, in that it is learned only as a result of sensory and perceptual contact with another person. The use of the term identification to describe this type of social learning is to be credited to Freud and the psychoanalytic school.

It seems clear that there are two forms of identification. Lair has made a very useful distinction between these two forms as they appear in psychological literature.[6] The first and most widely seen form she calls developmental identification. This form comes nearest

[6] Mowrer, op. cit., p. 590.

being what has often been called *imitation*. Here we find a child reproducing parts of the personality of the parent who is much loved without regard to the utility of the specific behavior. The loved parent is loved because many needs are met by him or her. The sight and sound and acts of the parent therefore come to be a sign of drive reduction through need satisfaction. The child engages in certain acts or makes certain sounds in order to have for its own satisfaction a small part of the loved and longed-for parent. A twelve-month-old girl reproduces for her own enjoyment certain parts of the behavior of her parents chiefly because these various acts occur almost simultaneously with the satisfaction of many of her primary needs. To put it crudely, she takes into herself parts of Father and Mother so she can have Father and Mother with her all the time even though they are at work or out hanging up laundry or whatever they may be doing which causes a physical separation.

The second form of identification is called by Lair *defensive identification*. It is this type that is commonly listed with the defense mechanisms in discussions of dynamic psychology. The idea that motivates this form is, "If you can't win over your aggressor, then swallow him." He won't be as dangerous and painful if you make him part of yourself as if he attacks you from outside. Even during the first year, parents try to teach a child that some things must be avoided because they are dangerous. When the baby reaches for an electrical outlet, the mother says, "No, Anne," frowns, shakes her

44

head. Sometimes this is enough, but it may be re-enforced by a light snapping of her fingers. The child then gets to the point where she reaches for the outlet, then frowns, shakes her head, withdraws her hand, and goes on to some other play project. She has incorporated a part of her parents' disapproval of electrical outlets as play spots into herself and shows this by frowning to herself and shaking her head when she approaches them. By doing this she defends herself against the parents' manifest disapproval. It is easy to go one step further. The parents do not normally frown and shake their heads as they approach electrical outlets. Nor does she later, but she no longer plays with them. A process of true defensive identification has now played its part in shaping one small segment of her character.

This very brief discussion should at least suggest some of the great potentialities for learning in both of these forms. The essential prerequisite for developmental identification is that the learner shall like and admire very much the object of identification. The *sine qua non* for defensive identification—which quite clearly is the avenue for major development of the superego or conscience of the person—seems to be a combination of emotional dependence and healthy respect for the object. An understanding of the importance of this factor in learning will make the choice of teachers in the program of either character education or religious education seem all the more grave a choice for the future of the children, for identification certainly influences not only overt acts but much more subtly the attitudes and ways of thinking about various problems.

C. Concept of self

Another factor in learning which is dynamic in effect is what has been variously called the *ego ideal* or the *concept of the self*. If we were thinking only of this factor we would want to look at the writings of Fritz Kunkel and of Carl Rogers. With the limited amount of space we may devote to this factor in personality development we will give attention only to the point of view of a little-known teacher and writer, Prescott Lecky. My introduction to the thought of Lecky was through Frederick C. Thorne in his then newly founded *Journal of Clinical Psychology*.[7] It seems almost paradoxical that Thorne, who started his journal as a corrective to the theory and practice of Rogers, should have so early written of Lecky who later seems to have profoundly influenced the school of psychotherapy of which Thorne was so critical.

Lecky's theory, as briefly and simply as possible, was that personality is not fixed or static but is progressively shaped, beginning at birth, by the new experiences which change existing ideas and attitudes. The single most important aspect of the personality is the concept of self which the individual holds. This concept is constantly changing—during childhood moving through such roles as Indian, cowboy, G-man, doctor, minister, bandit.

[7] "Directive Psychotherapy: II. The Theory of Self-Consistency," *Journal of Clinical Psychology*, I, 2 (April, 1945), p. 155.

Lecky believed that a normal personality is constantly striving to bring all of its parts and all that enters into it into unity. A process of selection of new elements goes on constantly. The selection of elements to be assimilated is determined by the concept of the self. In other words, only those new attitudes and behaviors are adopted which fit in with the individual's conception of his role in life.

Over a period of time a child builds up a conception of himself which leads to increasing internal consistency. This is done by assimilating ideas and attitudes which cause internal conflict. If a new idea is consistent with what is already present—and especially with the concept of the self—then it is easily and quickly accepted. If an inconsistent idea is presented it is rejected, or, if presented very forcibly, it may be assimilated and result in a conflict in the course of which existing ideas and attitudes are modified. From this standpoint, internal conflict is a natural function of the mind whose purpose is to work constantly to bring about an internal consistency between the ideas, attitudes, and behavior of the individual and the idea of the self which he holds. Lecky believed, therefore, that a moderate amount of conflict is essential for mental health.

It becomes obvious that this point of view is relevant to learning theory. Readiness to learn is particularly a function of the person's conception of himself. Best conditions for learning are present when (1) existing needs of the personality make it desirable or necessary to take in the new material, (2) when the new material is consistent with the rest of embodied past experience, (3) when there are no incompatible ideas or conceptions of the self to get in the way. Learning will go best when the person's conception of himself requires him to concentrate his abilities as much as possible. When a person who has failed continuously to use proved ability gets a proper and adequate conception of himself it is almost as though a miracle has taken place.

Evelyn was a college freshman who seemed promising but made consistently low grades on exams and was unable to enter into classroom discussions. The professor finally gave Evelyn an intelligence test, to discover she had an I. Q. of 139. As she talked with the professor about this figure and the level of her classwork she said, "But that can't be true because my father always said I was stupid." The teacher reassured her of her real ability. She left with a new concept of herself, and from that day on her scholastic progress was phenomenal.

In Bible-training-school class we sometimes have had students in mental hygiene who had much difficulty in learning the material. It was interesting to watch this process when the student was somewhat chiliastic in orientation and tried to struggle with the mental-health point of view which sometimes sees chiliasm as a form of escape from reality. There was real internal conflict. The unifying process at work centering in the self concept accomplished one of two things—either it rejected completely the mental-health point of view or it assimiliated

48

it and modified the other ideas until the internal conflict was resolved.

Another interesting observation of this order has been that as long as a seminarian thinks of himself solely as a student the practical courses in the curriculum have little interest for him and no significant learning takes place. As soon as we get him to see himself as a pastor or an educator, however, he is ready for significant progress in all the practical fields in a seminary curriculum.

The gang-age boy has little interest in knowing or in learning anything about personal grooming, but with the coming of adolescence there blossoms a concept of self as "a boy to whom a girl might say 'yes' if asked for a date." Now he learns rapidly what fits with his concept of himself. We have meant to say that the ego ideal or concept of the self has profound significance as a dynamic factor related to learning.

D. Social atmosphere in learning

Down through the years, there have been many individuals who have been painfully aware of the effect on general learning of a teacher who was primarily stern and forbidding. It must be admitted that there remains a strong element of authoritarianism in much of our education from elementary school up through many college and seminary courses. A. H. Maslow and Béla Mittelmann give some of the following marks of authoritarian education: (1) seeing the teacher as one who knows all, is all powerful, and makes no mistakes, (2) giving the teacher unquestioning obedience, (3) seeing the teacher as made of different stuff, not sharing in our own passions and struggle, (4) being punished frequently, (5) being humiliated in various ways in class, (6) pitting each student against every other student by giving grades, report cards, exams, (7) emphasizing learning by rote with no great concern for understanding.[8]

The effects of this kind of education on growing persons are quite varied, but one may justifiably raise the question of whether in general they are salutary. Wexberg gave the unlovely picture of what is often seen as the result of this practice in so-called learning situations. After describing how authoritarianism encourages students to do just what is required, to answer just what the teacher wants, never to question even the greatest nonsense, and hence to fail completely to develop the ability to think independently, Wexberg continued:

Life finishes what the home and the school began. Model children can hardly become anything more than employees, and if by chance they find themselves in independent situations the subaltern employee-nature of their essential being comes to the fore the more quickly. It would not matter if they were good employees! But they are the carriers of the most inconsolable bureaucracy, theirs is the greatest thought-laziness and the greatest shirking of all responsibility. They never accomplish anything, but they

[8] *Principles of Abnormal Psychology* (New York: Harper & Brothers, 1941), p. 224.

are artists in "passing the buck"; they interpret their duties always literally, never toward any independent purpose. Are they happy? We think not. Perhaps they are saved the grosser buffets of fate; failures and disappointments are not theirs so long as their employment goes its regular way without interruption. What they never experience is the pleasure of real accomplishment by their own performance, the pride of thinking their own thoughts! But if the model child who has been educated for the status of an employee is thrown out of his regular rut by some accident, then the happiness of his secure existence is at an end. He becomes the plaything of a capricious Fate, for he has lost the ability to act for himself (and he has no friends, for those who do only their duty seldom have many friends), and he finds himself completely unable to rebuild his life.[9]

All of this may be said to be anecdotal or an armchair commentary on the effects of the social atmosphere in which learning takes place. Although some of our own observation may confirm what has been said, we keep our tongues in our cheeks because of our experience with some seemingly happy results of the authoritarian approach.

The most significant (genuinely seminal in character), carefully designed experiments on the effect of the social atmosphere on learning were carried out a few years ago by Kurt Lewin and his students, especially Ronald Lip-

[9] E. Wexberg, Your Nervous Child (New York: Albert & Charles Boni, Inc.), pp. 102 ff. Used by permission.

pitt and Ralph K. White. The report of this research is genuinely worth reading for every educator and especially for those of us who call ourselves religious educators.[10]

The investigators attempted to discover the influence on personality of working in autocratic, democratic, and laissez-faire groups. The groups were club groups of boys with adult leaders who worked at various kinds of projects. A rather successful attempt was made to design the experimental set-up so that the differences in behavior which were due to the different "social atmosphere" of the group would be noted.

The results are interesting for all educators. Only a few of the most significant ones can be pointed out here. The cohesiveness of the group was much better in the democratic group. This was shown by more "we" remarks in proportion to "I" remarks. Reasons for lack of cohesiveness in the autocratic group were: (1) repeated and disturbing restriction of spontaneous movement by leader, (2) restriction of free and easy sociability among the boys, (3) sharp dichotomizing of what "he wants us to do and what we want to do." Dissatisfaction in laissez-faire groups arose chiefly from need for structure and presence of confusion and uncertainty due to the laissez-faire situation.

[10] Lewin, Lippitt, and White, "Patterns of Aggressive Behavior in Experimentally Created 'Social Climates'," *Journal of Social Psychology* (May, 1939), 10, pp. 271-99, and Lippitt and White, "The 'Social Climate' of Children's Groups," in Roger G. Barker, Jacob S. Kounin, and Herbert F. Wright, *Child Behavior and Development*, (New York: McGraw-Hill Book Company, 1943), pp. 485-508.

Another difference to be noted was the continued work when the leader was out of the room. The democratic groups showed only a slight drop. Both submissive and aggressive autocratic groups showed marked decline when the leader was out. There were about three times as many expressions of discontent in laissez-faire and submissive autocracies as in democratic groups, ten times as many in aggressive-autocratic groups. When the projects were completed in one autocratic club one object was presented to the leader and the others taken home to be used as decorations. In the democratic groups the boys tended to praise each other's efforts, while in the autocratic they became increasingly competitive for the praise of the adult autocratic leader.

In summary, it seems clear from these ingeniously designed experiments that in learning activity situations that are characterized by an authoritarian atmosphere much work may be done and skills may successfully be taught, but it is just as clear that some of the by-products are increased ego-centeredness, lack of identification with group goals, aggressive activity which tends to focus on "scapegoats," discontent with the activity, lack of pride in results that may show up in destruction of the products of the activity. In all of these areas the democratic learning situation shows up to an advantage over both the autocratic and the laissez-faire situations. What is indicated, therefore, is that in autocratically oriented learning situations, we might be studying democracy or Christian co-operation and be developing simultaneously

53

attitudes that are the exact opposites of democracy and Christian co-operation. Lewin, Lippitt, and White have done a splendid service in lifting up the effect of the social climate in which learning activities take place.

CONCLUSION

This chapter has not assumed that traditional discussions of learning are irrelevant to the work of the religious educator. The thesis is that these dynamic factors in the learning process are of such importance that they, too, must be understood and taken into account in making our plans. Specifically, it becomes clear (1) that if sublimation of sexual drives is necessary in order to release psychic energy for learning, parents and responsible adults must require the modification of the primitive sexual behavior of the child; (2) that if identification is an important factor, then the choice of teachers should take into account not only how well they know content material, or even how well they know child psychology, but that choice must be weighted heavily in terms of evaluation of *what kind of persons they are*, recognizing that if they are liked many of their characteristics will be taken over almost automatically by their pupils; (3) that one of the crucial tasks in all education that purports to influence emerging personality is to provide a concept of the self that will facilitate those learnings that seem desirable and will lead to the elimination of those qualities that are undesirable; and (4) that if we desire a co-operative and brotherly society our educational procedure must be based in a social climate which is democratic in the best sense of the word.

These dynamic factors are simple enough to be understood by any religious educator. They are profound enough in their implications to cause us to re-evaluate many of our procedures. They may be ignored only at the risk of defeating ourselves in the areas of our task that seem most important.

III

The Psychology of Group Process

A distinctive aspect of the educational segment of the church's life and work is that it is largely carried on in small groups. Preaching and corporate worship have usually been associated with large gatherings of the church. But in all the work of planning, in the study of the Bible, in the following of whatever curriculum may be prescribed—in all these the single most distinctive fact is that this takes place in groups of from five to twenty-five persons. Without any sophisticated theory to support it the church has discovered that there are many aspects of Christian nurture that can be carried on more satisfactorily in relatively small groups than in meetings of the whole.

Any careful observation of the meetings of these small groups in the average congregation will reveal that widely varying degrees of satisfaction and of accomplishment result from them. Some members may have entered a particular committee or board with some reluctance only to discover that they genuinely enjoy their work on it and would miss a meeting only because of necessity and with great regret. Some come to a particular meeting of a church-school class or discussion group with great anticipation and a real feeling of need but go away bitterly disappointed and with no desire to return. Some persons find that they feel warmly drawn to the members of a group but feel the meetings to be a waste of time in that nothing seems to get accomplished. Some members agree to serve on committees set up to meet real needs but feel frustrated and blocked in coming to any agreements.

What we have observed is that the presence of small groups of people is one of the most distinctive characteristics of Christian education, but that this particular aspect of the church's life is in itself characterized by the most widely varied ability to provide satisfactions for the members or to accomplish the purposes for which it exists.

Happily for the church, help is available from the social sciences. The study of group processes is a relatively recent phenomenon in the social-science field. As basic studies flow from social psychology and sociology, however, there has become available a body of data and principles that is applied in ever-widening circles of human relations—business administration, control of voluntary agencies, public administration, the miltary services, classroom management, administration of public education, leadership development in the church, et cetera. It is impossible in these few pages to make any adequate reference to the mass of basic research upon which the field of group development and dynamics is based. It is hoped that this may provide enough introduction that the value of the study of group dynamics for Christian education may be plain and the serious student stimulated to further study.

THE NATURE OF GROUPS

It seems quite satisfactory to define a group as "an aggregate of organisms in which the existence of all is utilized for the satisfaction of some needs of each." [1] In an ideal sense such a definition should cover all of the aggregations of persons who make up the Christian education aspect of the life of a congregation. If it is objected that not all such aggregations do indeed provide satisfaction for some needs of each, we would need to agree but with the hope that increasingly such groups will indeed meet some needs of each member. It is profitable to consider the nature of groups as did the research team headed by Cattell from the standpoint of population, structure, and syntality. [2]

A. Population of the group

Much of what a group will become, something of what it will accomplish, its ability to provide satisfactions for its members, its ability to maintain itself as a group— these and many other aspects of group life are heavily dependent upon the population characteristics of the group.

[1] Raymond B. Cattell, David R. Saunders, and Glen F. Stice, "The Dimensions of Syntality in Small Groups," A. Paul Hare, Edgar F. Borgatta, and Robert F. Bales (eds.), *Small Groups* (New York: Alfred A. Knopf, Inc., 1955), p. 306.

[2] *Ibid.*, p. 307.

The major questions here are, What kind of persons are these as persons? What kind of interests do they bring? What is their general level of intellectual ability? What special manual skills do they possess? What artistic or expressive gifts exist among them? What tendencies are there toward authoritarianism or domination among them? What needs for expression of love or aggression lie hidden within them? These questions all deal with inner and personal matters that will influence each person's participation in the life of a group.

Another order of questions that determine the nature of the population has to do with its membership in other groups and the consequent competing or conflicting loyalties that they bring into the group. Most persons hold membership in more than one group. Such groups may not be competitive in any way except in demand for the time of their members. On the other hand, it is quite likely that some members will hold membership in groups whose demands and standards are very much in conflict. These intergroup conflicts of ideals and standards will be internalized by the members and will almost inevitably cause erratic behavior. Some of the conflict and difficulty in group situations can be understood only by taking into account this overlapping and conflicting multiple membership. Even the establishment of a rational hierarchy of values and loyalties cannot completely eliminate the problems caused by conflicting multiple memberships. However, a knowledge of the existence and nature of such multiple memberships and their effects will cause group behavior to seem somewhat less irrational.

B. *Structure of the group*

The small groups which are related to Christian education vary greatly in their structure. Most standing committees have a fixed structure with a chairman whose duties may be more or less clearly understood but whose manner of operation is probably much less clearly defined. Various *ad hoc* committees may have much less formal organization. The classes or fellowship groups may vary from clearly defined and fairly rigid structures to almost no definable structures. They may have teachers who are authoritarian or teachers who are permissive and nondirective.

Current findings from social psychology would indicate that those people who need to be dependent and desire authority over them will prefer membership in groups that are characterized by authoritarian structure. The same devices of authoritarian rule may be seen in church groups that are found in political machines. Much emphasis on efficiency, denigration of discussion as the "pooling of ignorance," talk about undebatable moral issues while decisions about the common life are made by a select power group—these are characteristic of authoritarian structure no matter where the group is found.

Some groups are strictly bound by a constitution and bylaws which seem to impede progress toward a desired goal more than to facilitate such progress. Or such groups may find themselves bound within the straitjacket of a prearranged schedule, agenda, or program. Such previous planning or arrangements may help the group to accomplish its tasks if there is sufficient flexibility so that changes can be made in order to satisfy the needs of the participants.

It seems clear that the structure of the group should be determined by the purposes of the group. If the purposes of a group include the development in its members of the disposition and ability to participate in a democratic society, the cultivation of sensitivity to the rights and the worth of each individual, the development of a practical expression of love in group relationships, then the group must develop a structure which enhances the worth of each individual and provides an opportunity for each to exercise his own capabilities. It seems most likely that the participative group structure will contribute most to the accomplishment of such purposes.

C. *Syntality of the group*

Every group has its own distinctive characteristics apart from the summation of the characteristics of the individuals making up the group. Cattell has chosen the term *syntality* for this dimension of group life as a term analogous to *personality* as a dimension of the life of the person. In a massive and rigorously designed and executed study of this dimension of group life he found fourteen factors making up the syntality of the eighty groups he studied. These factors were found by factor analysis, and the naming of them is subject to the difficulty which is always inherent in naming a statistical reality derived from factor analysis. Those which have been tentatively named by Cattell are:

1. Vigorous unquestioned purposefulness vs. self-conscious unadaptedness
2. Immediate high synergy [group interest and energy] vs. low motivation
3. Democratic, explicit procedure-orientation vs. horde urgency
4. Schizothyme rigidity vs. conformity to circumstances [Central feature: High and unadaptable aspiration level]
5. High intrinsic synergy vs. low intrinsic synergy
6. Intelligent role interaction vs. low morale
7. Democratic "savoir faire" vs. lack of self possession
8. High verbal interaction
9. Recklessness
10. Group elation vs. group phlegm
11. Homogeneity of emotional maturity
12. Disregard of group vs. acceptance of group goals
13. Frustrating temperamental heterogeneity vs. morale from homogeneity
14. Diffidence in internal communications.[3]

It is proposed by the investigators that some of the syntality factors present significant correlations with the personality factors of the group populations but that there seem to be some emergents in syntality that are the product of certain combinations of personalities.

[3] *Ibid.* See pp. 319-28.

Many words have been used to describe groups with some empirical validity. From a rigorous statistical point of view Cattell's dimensions seem most satisfactory.

LEADERSHIP IN GROUPS

Leadership has often been described in terms of personality traits. When thought of in these terms it is something that some people have and that others do not. The search for leaders then consists of seeking out those people who have these traits in the highest degree. Burt has said that leadership is a concept applied to the relation between person and environment when one person is so placed that his will, feeling, and insight direct and control others in the pursuit of a cause.[4] Actually the current understanding of leadership is somewhat different from these and many of the traditional ideas. Leadership is currently conceived as a function of the structure of a group. There is a division of labor within the group in which each member carries his own responsibilities, and the movement of the group toward its goals is dependent upon the function of each member.

A. *Psychoanalytic theory of leader and group formation*

A psychoanalytic approach to group formation was worked out by Fritz Redl in terms of the kind of cen-

[4] Cecil A. Gibb, "The Principles and Traits of Leadership," *Ibid.*, p. 88.

tral figure providing leadership for the group. In his working out of these leadership types in group formation he dealt primarily with the emotions of the members as these are handled by the various defense mechanisms elaborated by the personality. Ten different types of focal person are described.

1. The "Patriarchal Sovereign": The conscience part of the superego of the central person is incorporated by the group members. The group members want to behave in such a way as to be approved by the central person. This causes enough similarity that they get along well together.

2. The "Leader": The personality of the central person is incorporated in the ego-ideal portion of the superego of the members. On the basis of the resulting similarity the members develop feelings of warmth toward each other.

3. The "Tyrant": The values of the central person are incorporated by the members due to fear. The end product is the same as type 1 but the motivation is different.

4. The "Love Object": The central person does not have his values internalized by the members. The members are integrated by a non-threatening type of sexual love for him.

5. The "Object of Aggressive Drives": The central person here cannot accurately be spoken of as a leader. It is the focusing of the aggressive drives of the members on this person that integrates the group.

6. The "Organizer": The central person provides a service to the ego of the members by showing means of enjoying forbidden pleasures and minimizing their own feelings of guilt and anxiety. There is no love, hatred, or identification with the central figure.

7. The "Seducer": The central person integrates the group by performing an act for the first time which may be representative of repressed desires of all members. He thus reduces their own feelings of guilt and makes it easier for them to over-ride their own superegos.

8. The "Hero": The central person provides a service to the ego of the members by performing the first act of a kind that is good and morally justifiable but that the members have been hindered from doing by their own cowardice. Thus by the initiatory act of the Hero the submissive tendencies of the members are overcome.

9. The "Bad Influence": The central person is one whose behavior is not inhibited by conscience and he pursues his socially forbidden course with no feelings of guilt. He thus saves the members from guilt feelings by infecting them with his own unconflicted personality. Thus the latent undesirable drives of the members come to be openly expressed.

10. The "Good Example": The group members who have undesirable drives which threaten their equilibrium are assisted by the example of a central person who is unconflicted. He infects them in the direction of moral values. He thus helps to strengthen the superegos of the threatened members and through a common solution of conflict the members are drawn to each other.[5]

Redl summarizes the situation by showing that the ten types can be placed in three categories on the basis of the role of the focal person in the process of group for-

[5] See Fritz Redl, "Group Emotion and Leadership," *ibid.*, pp. 71-86.

mation: (1) an object of identification, either from love or from fear; (2) an object of drives, either of love or of aggression; and (3) an ego support, either through providing means for drive satisfaction or by dissolving conflict through removal or easing of guilt.

This analysis is a very perceptive one in the study of all kinds of groups and the leadership within them which determines their nature.

Current leadership theory[6]

The first emphasis in leadership theory is that the emergence of leadership is always relative to the social situation. It is the nature of the social situation that determines what specific personality characteristics are called for in the person or persons that will be best able to assist the group in the marshaling of its resources to satisfy the most needs of the members. One social situation may put a premium upon inventiveness, another upon social effectiveness in resolving conflict between members, another on stimulating the release of the energies of the members.

The second emphasis or principle is that the function of any individual in a leadership role is dependent upon the goal of the group and upon that individual's ability to contribute to the movement of the group toward its goal. Here one finds a real impasse between those who hold that the leader is always a product of the situation of the moment and those who hold that some people

---

[6] See Gibb, "*Principles and Traits of Leadership*," *ibid.*, pp. 90-94.

do genuinely influence the social situation of which they are a part. I am inclined toward the position that there is a sufficient truth in both views that to ignore either would seriously miss a full appreciation of this dimension of leadership.

The third principle is that leadership is basically a matter of social interaction. Leaders do not exist without followers; leader and followers are united by common purposes; the leader shares in membership. At the same time that the leader shares membership, however, he must be unique enough in some aspect to be able to facilitate the group's movement in that area toward its purposes. It must be noted that it is only as the leader sufficiently reflects the desires and purposes of the group that in a sense he is formed by the group that he qualifies for leadership.

These principles taken together could move one to accept Pigors' definition of leadership as a process of mutual stimulation which by the interplay of relevant differences channels human energy toward the satisfaction of a common purpose. Murray G. Ross and Charles E. Hendry think these theories are not adequate in themselves, that one must also take account of the organization within which leadership is to function, the social climate of the time, and the value system of the group that determines the leadership pattern.[7]

[7] *New Understandings of Leadership* (New York: Association Press, 1957), pp. 32-36.

B. *Leadership roles required*[8]

Whether one speaks of leader roles or group roles perhaps does not matter so long as it is clear that every group needs certain roles performed if it is to move toward its goals. The following are some that are imperative:

1. Calling for data: "Does anyone know what the facts are?"

2. Information giving: "The study we have just completed shows . . ."

3. Clarifying: "Do I hear you correctly as saying . . .?"

4. Arbitrating: "Could both values be saved by . . . ?"

5. Progress evaluating: "It seems that we are of one mind as to what we want to accomplish but are not yet agreed how."

6. Summarizing: "We seem to have said (1) . . .,(2) . . ., (3) . . . , and (4) . . . ."

All these roles help the group to move toward its goal. As the group works at its task it will need several other roles that assist it in maintaining its own unity.

1. Encourager: "That is a very helpful point you just made."

2. Good listener: "What you are saying interests me greatly." (Communicated without words.)

3. Tension reducer: "We are sort of like . . . (funny joke)."

These roles are only typical of the kind of things that need to be done for the sake of the group life. It could

---

[8] See Kenneth D. Benne and Paul Sheats, "Functional Roles of Group Members," *Journal of Social Issues*, IV, 2 (1948), pp. 41-49.

be said that anyone who performs any of these roles is taking a leadership role. Or we could say that many groups need no leader if these necessary roles are carried by various group members.

Looking at the whole matter of leadership for groups we see quite clearly that it is a real step forward to learn more about the leadership roles that are required and to see some of the advantages in participative groups in which the leadership roles are widely distributed among the group members rather than held tightly within the control of one or two people. It seems only realistic to observe, however, that most groups in the Christian-education program will have some central leadership position such as a chairman of a committee, a teacher of a class, a leader of a club. These leadership positions cannot and probably should not be eliminated, but the persons in them should be helped to see the value of the distribution of some of the roles to other members of the group.

FACTORS AFFECTING THE SATISFACTION IN AND SUCCESS OF GROUPS

We suggested at the beginning that not all groups yield satisfaction to their members, nor do all succeed in moving toward their goals. We should look briefly at some of the factors that influence the satisfaction and success of groups.

A. *Communication patterns*

Failure of communication between the members of a group is a serious deterrent to group satisfaction or movement. From the field of psychotherapy Carl Rogers brings the insight that a major barrier to communication is the tendency to judge and evaluate what the other person says. Rogers adds that the stronger the emotions involved the more likely we are to make evaluations and the less mutuality there is in the attempts at communication.

Rogers suggests as an answer to this barrier to communication that each person work hard to see an idea from the other's point of view, to feel as he feels about it, to achieve his frame of reference. This is the essence of nondirective therapy and simultaneously of communication.[9]

A simple way in which groups ban the evaluative element temporarily is in "brainstorming" or "taking the collection" where every person's contribution is accepted without any examination of its worth. This is done in order to get an unrestricted flow of all the ideas people may have. They are evaluated later—after they have become the property of the entire group.

Another thing that must be said about communication is that in one sense it is communication only if there is mutuality in it, only if it is two-way. Narrowly speaking, it may be held that communication can take place from one person to a group, but the research of Harold J. Leavitt and Ronald A. H. Mueller seems to indicate that feedback to the communicator increases the ac-

---

[9] Rogers and F. J. Roethlisberger, "Barriers and Gateways to Communication," *Harvard Business Review*, XXX, 4 (1952), pp. 46-52.

curacy of transmission, the confidence of the sender in formulating his messages.[10] The incorporation into group life of various provisions for feedback or two-way communication seems likely to add satisfaction.

The recognition that effective communication takes place at other than the verbal level is of first importance. The facial expression, the posture of the body, where one sits, the tone of voice—these are only a few examples of nonverbal communication that may either re-enforce or belie the words that are spoken. To understand the nonverbal communication of others and to be aware of one's own nonverbal communication almost certainly leads to more mature participation in groups.

Member satisfactions are enhanced if the functioning chairman permits the discussion to emerge as a general pattern of interaction (Figure 1) rather than as a series of interactions between himself and various group members (Figure 2). Participation charts for mature groups with a high level of satisfaction from general communication show many remarks directed to the entire group rather than to a single individual. (See Figure 3.)

B. Seating

It is not without significance that in the design of the building and meeting rooms for the United Nations, the most ambitious attempt at resolving tensions in world

[10] "Some Effects of Feedback on Communication," Hare, Borgatta, and Bales, *op. cit.*, pp. 414-23.

Free general communication

Figure 1

history, the most careful attention was given to the arrangement of the seating.

The rather simple but very interesting study by Bernard Steinzor revealed that in small groups the members sitting opposite each other are more likely to respond to each other than those sitting closer.[11] This is explained as being due to response to factors other than the word content—factors which are most effective when the person is in full view.

It is a matter of empirical observation that attitudes of rejection toward a group member will show up in

[11] "The Spatial Factor in Face to Face Discussion Groups," *ibid.*, pp. 348-53.

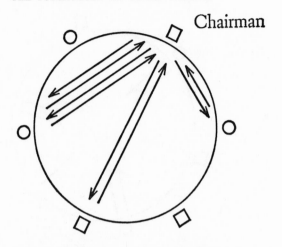

Restricted communication

Figure 2

seating arrangement and will affect the participation of the rejected member. The result may be withdrawal from participation or the development of overtalkative and aggressive behavior.

Formal seating in row after row tends to recall those situations with similar seating where there was no expectation of two-way communication. Participation by the group except in a questioning form becomes quite unlikely.

Seating around a table with room for note pads, tools, books, exhibits, and materials suggests a sharing of the

73

Remarks directed to the entire group

Figure 3

work and responsibility and facilitates the involvement of the total group.

Seating which separates the leader from the other members in position or level will increase the psychological distance and make genuinely participative group endeavor more difficult.

We have suggested only that the arrangement of seating for a group is usually representative of the leader-group relation or the psychological climate. It follows, however, that the modification of seating is one effective way to change the leader-group relation and psychological climate.

C. Size

No absolute number has been clearly stated as the optimum size of a group. H. A. Thelen stated a sound principle when he concluded that the group should always be the smallest possible group which can contain all the socialization and achievement skills required for doing the task.[12]

The studies of Robert F. Bales and Edgar F. Borgatta suggested many tentative conclusions about size that seem to be related to two gross factors involved in increasing size: (1) relative talking time becomes more limited as group size increases, and (2) each person is faced with a larger number of persons with whom he must maintain relationship and with less time to do it.[13]

Experienced discussion leaders point to the difficulty of conducting a good discussion with more than twelve to fifteen members. Part of the difficulty lies in the forces mentioned by Bales and Borgatta. It becomes increasingly difficult to be sensitive to individual needs, attention to which is so important to group maintenance, as size increases. Even in groups of fifteen to eighteen it will be profitable periodically to divide into groups of three to six for brief periods of discussion.

D. Balance of task and maintenance orientation

For a group to experience satisfaction and get its work

[12] "Group Dynamics in Instruction: Principle of Least Group Size," *School Review*, 57 (1949), pp. 139-48.

[13] "Size of Group as a Factor in the Interaction Profile," Hare, Borgatta, and Bales, *op. cit.*, pp. 396-413.

done there must be a healthy balance between certain devices and orientation which serves to maintain the group as a social organism and a genuine commitment to accomplish the task for which the group came into being.

The task of a "kaffeeklatsch" may be just that, and its maintenance may coincide with its task. But a group of couples planning a study course for their age may best do their work by taking time for "coffee and" in order to build and maintain the group as it works at its task. A balance in orientation seems most promising.

E. *Clearly stated goal*

A group may save its members much frustration if it makes certain that its task is clearly stated and is understood and accepted by the members. Only dissatisfaction and waste of time can result from a failure in these conditions. A clear statement of task or purpose should be a part of the invitation to join a group so that the acceptance of purpose is an integral aspect of membership.

F. *Leadership team*

A balanced and competent leadership team with all necessary role functions provided contributes greatly to member satisfactions and to group goal-directed activity. It is not to be assumed that because human-relations training uses as a central training device T-groups which are characterized by lack of designated leaders, agenda, or procedures, democratically functioning groups should operate likewise. The ordinary responsible group will have a person whose task it is to state the purpose of the meeting, define the issue, initiate discussion, state the consensus. It is quite true that in a mature group many of these functions will be wholly or in part carried by the members.

A necessary member of the leader team for many groups is a person to make some form of summary or running account of what the group thought and decided. The decisions may be part of an overall action program of a larger group or may be policy decisions for the future of the group itself. In any case, the recorder functions, under whatever name, must be provided for.

Out of the study of the dynamics of group process has emerged the concept of the observer of process.[14] Such a person who functions analytically and nonjudgmentally may be of inestimable value to a group by helping it see where it may be hung up and what may be needed to improve its own performance.

CONCLUSION

There is no satisfactory place to stop in considering the psychology of group processes. What we have hoped to do is to give enough introduction that readers will wish to study more and find their service in Christian education enhanced.

[14] J. R. Gibb, G. N. Platts, and L. F. Miller, *Dynamics of Participative Groups* (University of Delaware, Newark, Del.: J. R. Gibb, 1951), Chapter 8.

A final word of commendation could be said in behalf of certain current writing which gives more extended consideration of group process for the work of the church.[15] This, if added to some of the better more general writing in the field, will be of great assistance to the person working in Christian education.

[15] Casteel, John L. (ed.), *Spiritual Renewal Through Personal Groups* (New York: Association Press, 1957). Douglass, Paul F., *The Group Workshop Way in the Church* (New York: Association Press, 1956). Raines, Robert A., *New Life in the Church* (New York: Harper & Brothers, 1961).

IV

Psychological Development as a Factor in Religious Readiness

The Christian would sturdily resist the idea that the existence of God is in any sense dependent upon the experiences that people have. He believes that the Church, the Bible, truth, justice, and beauty will continue to be realities totally apart from the presence or absence of experience in individual persons. But the Christian will affirm just as sturdily that the past experiences of a person or his present state of development will profoundly affect the way in which he perceives God or any of these lesser aspects of reality.

Freud's reference to religion as being rooted in the dependency of a child on his father which is projected on a cosmic scale contains a profound element of truth. No person perceives or experiences God apart from the way in which his life has been formed by the relationships with his own father and mother. This is only to say that no person ever comes to any new experience or perception in a vacuum. He brings to any perception or to any new experience all that has happened to him in the past and all that he now is.

It is for this reason, which seems so trite and obvious in

79

statement, that a realistic approach to the teaching of religion can be made only as the educator uses what knowledge is available to him regarding the characteristics of the personality in its successive stages of development and the developmental tasks that must be completed in order for the person to pass successfully out of a stage. As he looks at the nature of the personality at a certain stage and discovers the tasks faced by the person, he begins to see some of the implications for the teaching of religion.

To speak of what it is to teach religion or to develop faith appropriate to the need of the person is to be primarily interested in the kind of authentic experience in which there is encounter between the person and God. We believe that this is the most real thing that ever happens to a person. It is the original I-Thou encounter for any individual. To look at it from the standpoint of God is to see it with God as the "I" who speaks to a person as a "Thou." To look at it from our view is to see the person as an "I" who meets the Ultimate in personal form, which is God, as "Thou." This results in the formation in the person of the Spirit as God is introjected, in the same manner that the introjection of the father figure results in the formation of the conscience or superego, or the ego ideal. Or if it is the response of the person through identification with the God who is encountered it results in the formation of spirit spelled with a small "s."

If we use theological language we can say that from

God's view what transpires is that he reaches out in grace to a person. From a person's view it is that he reaches out to God in faith. The fact that is clear is that this experience of encounter or of the grace-faith trans-action cannot be commanded by us at any time. About the best that we are able to do is to achieve some knowl-edge of the conditions under which God extends his grace and the conditions under which growing persons in all the varied stages of development are most likely to be open to the encounter. Then we try to provide the con-ditions under which the person and the Almighty meet each other. It is to this end that we examine the char-acteristics of the personality at its various stages and the tasks that it faces. Thus we can see something of the openness of the personality to the most significant event that can ever happen for that person—the God-man encounter in which a new person comes into being.

This is the way, then, in which we will look at the suc-cessive stages of development from the formative years of the young child to the senior years of life.

Susan Jones at three months was a happy and secure little girl. She had learned that when she became uncomfortable because of hunger or wetness or from being awake and alone a small cry was enough expression of her discomfort to be met by a kind, smiling, and warm person who held her, fed her, talked to her, and gave her such a deliciously satisfying feeling. At two and three years Susan learned that Mother expected her to begin to gain control over her own muscles and especially over her processes of elimination. At six years of age Susan became much in love with her father and sometimes resented her mother's special place in Daddy's life. Daddy firmly helped her to understand that he loved her but that Mother would continue to keep the special place as wife. At eleven it seemed to Susan as though she were coming apart because she was beginning to have so many feelings that she had long forgotten. Then in the next several years she felt a special call to love God. She also found herself much attracted to and stirred by some of the boys she knew. Susan at twenty-four had her first baby. There was a new warmness and tenderness in her which she felt not only for her husband but also for her baby. Susan at forty-eight saw the last of her three children leave home and had strange feelings of change within her own organism. She tried to find new sources of meaning for her life. At sixty-eight Susan and her husband, now retired, sold their home, bought a trailer, and moved to California to a community of people mostly their age. She and her husband had some hobbies they liked, but they did not quite feel needed as they had earlier.

Susan was the same person at each of the stages we have described with just a sentence. Yet in another sense at each stage she had different characteristics, different needs, and different tasks that needed to be completed. Susan Jones and Bob Smith are the people who make up our churches—each with his distinctive needs and backgrounds as he comes to those experiences which the church seeks to provide.

In our discussion of personality development we will draw heavily upon the writing and work of such psychoanalysts as Oliver S. English and Gerald H. J. Pearson, Irene M. Josselyn, E. H. Erikson.[1] The basic work on developmental tasks has been done by Robert J. Havighurst from whom basic data is taken for this integrative chapter.[2] S. M. Corey and J. E. Herrick have also written in this area.[3] In the area of religious readiness it is difficult to know how to divide the credit for ideas that have matured during the reading of Lewis J. Sherrill, Basil A. Yeaxlee, Reuel Howe, and others to a lesser degree.[4]

THE FORMATIVE YEARS—BIRTH TO 5½

A. Personality development

The first year of life is a time for the establishment of strong feelings of security in the new child by prompt and full satisfaction by devoted parents of needs for food,

[1] English and Pearson, *Emotional Problems of Living* (Rev. ed.; New York: W. W. Norton & Company, 1955). Josselyn, *The Happy Child* (New York: Random House, 1955). Erikson, *Childhood and Society* (New York: W. W. Norton & Company, 1950), Chapter 7.

[2] *Developmental Tasks and Education* (2nd ed.; New York: Longmans, Green & Company, 1952).

[3] Jerome Martin Seidman (ed.), *The Child: A Book of Readings* (New York: Holt, Rinehart, & Winston, Inc., 1958), pp. 31-41.

[4] Sherrill, *The Struggle of the Soul* (New York: The Macmillan Company, 1951). Yeaxlee, *Religion and the Growing Mind* (Greenwich, Conn.: The Seabury Press, 1952). Howe, *The Creative Years* (Greenwich, Conn.: The Seabury Press, 1959).

sucking, and fondling. It is by the taking in of food and by experience of the gentle care of the skin that the child achieves the feeling of being loved. This will affect all later relationships with people, and perhaps with God.

The second and third years will be years of learning to conform to the expectations of the culture of which mother and father are the most intimate representatives. This involves such matters as reasonable cleanliness of body and clothes and some polite attention to adult friends of the family. The symbol and perhaps most intimate demand of all of these is the learning of control of bowel and bladder functions. Here one finds the beginnings of the realization of the self as separate from mother. There is ego development and the dawning of ambivalence, or the ability simultaneously to love and hate the same person.

In the fourth to the sixth or seventh years there is the localization of a considerable portion of the pleasurable sensations in the genital areas. This is accompanied by and reciprocally related to almost universal masturbation during these years. It is notably the time of the family romance in which a child desires for himself as a love object the parent of the opposite sex. The renunciation of this desire usually leads to the beginning of real identification with the parent of the same sex.

B. Developmental tasks

The developmental tasks of this period are perhaps as complex and difficult for the child as any later tasks for the more mature person. They are (1) learning to walk—later to hop, skip and run, (2) learning to handle solid foods, (3) learning to talk, (4) learning control of elimination, (5) learning sex differences and sex modesty, (6) achieving physiological stability—temperature, metabolism rate, et cetera, (7) forming simple concepts of reality—big, black, dog, (8) learning to relate emotionally to other people, (9) learning to distinguish right and wrong and the development of a conscience.

These are the required tasks of the formative years. The child is biologically ready for them, the culture requires them, and psychologically the child in a normal situation moves happily toward their accomplishment.

C. Religious significance

The most important thing that happens to the child during these years is not the formal teaching about religion but the development of an attitude of basic confidence and trust. This will emerge from dependable care by warm and giving persons. In this the child learns the very basis for an understanding of and relationship to God. Here is the foundation of the faith response to God.

There is also here the dawn of the idea of the living of one's life under the necessity of certain demands. May we not assume that in the facing of the requirements of the culture—on the basis of a relationship of love from one's parents—the child finds it possible to see God as related to both love and structure (law)?

MIDDLE CHILDHOOD YEARS 5½ TO 10½

There is no term for this period that is completely satisfactory. Our choice is perhaps not the best one, and we will use it sparingly.

A. *Personality development*

Completion of the dynamic structure of the psyche comes about in this period. Last to be added is the full conscience or superego which emerges primarily from the solution of the problem posed by the family romance— the child now accepting the sexual standards of the culture regarding incest relationships. Friends become much more important than parents. In the former period it was found necessary to give up the parent; now the peers are the substitutes. Great conformity is required. The age is naturally homosexual in that each sex prefers its own sex for companionship.

There is often considerable hostility and rebellion that can be mobilized in such groups. This is probably displaced hostility left over from the solution of the family romance problem.

There is a strong need for ideal persons with whom the child can identify. The character of the status persons in his environment is of the utmost importance. The surrender of his own internal drives leads to the need for these objects of introjection. Children of this age are ready to do work if the work can be an opportunity to share with and have time with an admired person.

B. Developmental tasks

This age is noted for its thrust out of the family into the peer group, the physical thrust into work and play, and the mental thrust into the world of adult mental processes and communication. These are the developmental tasks of the middle years: (1) learning physical skills necessary for common games, (2) building wholesome attitudes toward oneself as growing organism— e.g., care of body, enjoying use of the body, (3) learning to get along with age-mates—to make friends and get along with enemies, (4) learning to be one's own sex with its appropriate role, (5) developing skills in reading, writing, and calculating, (6) developing concepts necessary for everyday living—e.g., time, space, number, (7) developing conscience, morality, and a scale of values, (8) achieving personal independence—ability to plan and act independently of parents or other adults, (9) developing social attitudes that are basically democratic.

C. Religious significance

There is much significance in the relation of the child to the church. This middle-years child wants a group and gives supreme loyalty to it. Its nature will be instrumental in the formation of his conscience. There is danger here. Dostoevski has the Grand Inquisitor say to Jesus, "This craving for community of worship is the chief misery of every man individually and of humanity from the beginning of time." [5]

[5] *The Brothers Karamazov.*

He wants people who can be his ideals. Teachers, club leaders, his minister, admirable characters in biography and story—all of these, if chosen carefully, will be influential in making a healthy Christian person.

Like the parent, the church must not be too possessive. It should recognize that, like the child's parents, it cannot meet his every need. Some will best be met elsewhere. Sherrill insists that in the Biblical view, the church is never mother nor father, but is a family, a household, a brotherhood. These concepts will more nearly fit the type of relationship which the middle-years child needs.

ADOLESCENCE

A. *Personality development*

Usually adolescence is thought of as the period beginning with puberty and gradually merging into maturity. Sometimes a prepuberty stage (ages 10-12) is pointed out as the merging end at the beginning. This is characterized by changing relationships with members of the opposite sex. There are obvious bids for attention, but they will be in the form of giggling or horseplay. There is a growth spurt not only physically but also in terms of erotic sensitivity. The preadolescent may be well-nigh flooded with these deepened sensory experiences. A defense against this may be seen in alternation between periods of great alertness and sensitivity and periods of apathy and disinterestedness. This looks like moodiness but disappears as the growth spurt evens out. Crushes on slightly older peers or adults are common as the prepubertal child turns almost entirely away from parents. As a safeguard against renewal of the family romance with its hurt the girl tends to become very disagreeable to the father, the boy to the mother. This may alternate with a genuine renewal of the romance with very intimate approaches to the parent of the opposite sex.

In postpuberty or late adolescence the person has a real need to (1) have made a decision on his life work, (2) find a means to pay for training in it, and (3) develop genuine enthusiasm for it. He also needs to become emancipated from the parents. Certain factors stand in the way of such emancipation: (1) the emotional need to be cared for, (2) reluctance to accept responsibility, (3) fear of criticism if responsibility is taken, and (4) lack of desire to serve and co-operate with adults. There are matching difficulties to be found in adults which make emancipation difficult.

Perhaps most important in this period is the development of significant and maturing heterosexual relationships. An open, frank, trusting attitude from the parents accompanied by many opportunities for heterosexual association is ideal. When this is accompanied by discussions between parents and adolescents about the standards and ideals of the parents, things usually turn out well. English and Pearson concluded their discussion on adolescence by saying:

We are telling our young people too little about life. They should be going out into the world with an urge to help, to give, to create, to care for and to care about. Only in this way will they find their existence emotionally rewarding and satisfying over and above economic and social success.[6]

B. Developmental tasks

The principal areas of task are emotional and social, not intellectual. The developmental tasks are (1) achievement of more mature relations with age-mates of both sexes—seeing girls as women, boys as men—learning to associate with others on a mature basis, (2) acceptance of and effective use of the body, (3) acceptance and living out of an adult masculine or feminine role that is socially approved, (4) achievement of emotional independence of parents while still being able to retain affection for them, (5) achievement of assurance of being able to make a living, (6) selection of and preparation for an occupation for which one has necessary ability, (7) development of a positive attitude toward family life and having children and the necessary skills in family management, (8) development of intellectual skills necessary for participation in democratic government, (9) participation as a responsible adult in the life of the community, region, and nation, (10) acquiring of a set of values and an ethical system as a guide to behavior.

C. Religious significance

It is at this time of emancipation and moving into a new selfhood that youth stand in danger of being caught

[6] *Op. cit.*, p. 352.

up in the promises of that which is "not-God." The claims of science, the pull of things, the demands of patriotism, the necessity to conform—all these reach out to seize the adolescent just emerging into freedom and to subject him to an unworthy slavery of the total person. The gospel to youth is that "a new creation" is intended in him by God. This is a work of love profoundly exemplified in Christ, and faith is the outgoing love to and commitment of life to God in return.

The weaning from the emotional sovereignty of the parents opens the way to take on the sovereignty of God. Sherrill points to four common types of response: (1) change from human to divine sovereignty, (2) external conformity with no inner difference or even active resentment against God's claims, (3) rebellion against any part of the church, God himself, or simply against religion as a symbol of the parents, (4) no response, leaving youth seeking fulfillment in "non-God."

THE YOUNG ADULT 18-30

A. Personality development

"Early adulthood is the most individualistic period of life and the loneliest one, in the sense that the individual, or, at the most, two individuals, must proceed with a minimum of social attention and assistance to tackle the most important tasks of life," said Havighurst.[7] The early years of young adulthood are extremely ego centered. Both the man and woman are very much involved in

[7] *Op. cit.*, pp. 72-73.

making right decisions that will provide for a satisfying future. Yet there is often a strong feeling of inadequacy for the making of such decisions and the young adult finds little help or guidance. The need for approval, for a feeling of acceptance, for recognition of worth, is very great. The person has moved from a period of age grouping to social-status grouping. This makes the matter of status loom very large. In this adult culture the person finds that status and approval "depend not so much on age as on skill and strength and wisdom, and family connections." [8] Satisfaction in a job is not entirely dependent upon pay but upon the feeling of worth as a total person that comes from the job. Satisfaction in marriage derives not just from whether the mate is beautiful or handsome but from the lack of tension and the reduction of anxiety that is to be found in the companionship and the joint enterprise with the beloved. Children are seen as a visible result of love and at the same time as a demonstration of the ability to perpetuate what the individual holds to be of value.

B. Developmental tasks

To list the tasks of this period is relatively simple. (1) Selecting a mate is the most interesting, disturbing, and absorbing of tasks; other tasks are (2) learning to live with a marriage partner in such a way as to at once fulfill each other's lives and build a happy relationship, (3) having children successfully, (4) rearing children in such

[8] *Ibid.*, p. 73.

a way as to meet their deepest needs, (5) managing a home as a function of the husband, wife, or partnership, (6) getting started in an occupation, (7) taking on a civic responsibility—neighborhood, community group, church, et cetera, (8) finding a congenial social group in which leisure-time activities can be patterned.

C. Significance of religion

This is a time of far-reaching and significant choice with regard to what the ego will do with the claim of God upon his life. Whether this is a time of original commitment and reorganization of the self in relation to God or the coming of the mature search for the significance of all areas of life in the presence of God does not seem to matter too much. The basic question is whether God and one's commitment to him shall constitute a small compartment in one's life or whether God is permitted to confront and bring into being a new creation in every area of the young adult's functioning. There is a temptation to accept the assurance of the gospel without opening the self to its claims.

How does the church look to young adults? Sherrill sees the church in four ways. (1) It is home—especially for the unmarried adults who have found freedom but need comradeship and fellowship at a genuine level. It is also home for some who are near disaster and need support. (2) It is attainment in that when it embodies the concept of acceptance by faith it relieves the struggling person of the necessity of perfection of character,

93

church, creed, or Christian experience as a basis of acceptance. When love of God is perfect in the church people are accepted on faith. (3) It is seen as enlargement in that the self is enlarged and expanded by its identification with a dynamic group. (4) It is seen as self-correcting in that in it Jesus Christ and the Word of God confront man and his institutions and make their corrective demands.

MIDDLE AGE

A. Personality development

Maturity is a time when it is easy to let the circle of friends constrict because it takes effort to keep friendships alive. Perhaps the greatest support is found when a middle-aged couple have a minimum of four close friends.

Relation to the families of each child will be dependent almost entirely on how the family got along as children and the degree to which the parents have been able to cut themselves free. English and Pearson said, "Parents should do all they can to enjoy their children when they are young and in their teens so that when marriage comes they can relinquish them to their mates." [9]

Some middle-aged people are seldom seen in the community. Others take part only in those activities which can give pleasure. Still others carry major responsibility in the life of a community. Not only is such activity needed by the community, but it seems likely such ac-

[9] *Op. cit.,* p. 424.

tivity keeps people younger, more optimistic, more flexible, and less likely to be lonely and a problem to others as they grow older.

The menopause causes emotional difficulties for some women. Those having severe trouble tend to be women who were sensitive and lived in isolation, those who declare they never visit much but stay home and mind their own business, who have made a virtue of their fear of people or their dislike for people, who are pedantic in the training of children, who are excessively religious, who are meticulous about cleanliness, who are sexually frigid, who are ungenerous and critical. Women need not go through such experiences, but the prevention lies in the way the child is reared.

Men may have some of the same anxiety, but such anxiety is purely a psychological phenomenon as over against the partially physically based phenomenon in the woman. Sometimes men do become concerned about ageing and "their waning powers." They may then attempt by silly and inappropriate activity to demonstrate their continuing vitality and masculinity.

B. Developmental tasks

This is a period when men and women reach the peak of their influence upon society and in which society makes maximum demands upon them. Both men and women are acting reciprocally within a family situation in which there are "teeners." The tasks are (1) achieving of adult civic and social responsibility, (2) establishing and maintaining of an economic standard of living involving the participation of the entire family, (3) assisting teen-age children to become responsible and happy adults, (4) developing of adult leisure-time activities that can be sources of satisfaction in later years, (5) renewal of relating to one's spouse as a beloved after the years of concentration on mothering and on making a niche in business or profession, (6) accepting and adjusting to the physiological changes of middle age, (7) adjusting to ageing parents in such ways as to make a satisfying old age for them and provide happiness for the middle-aged generation.

C. Religious significance

Sherrill sees as the most significant religious task of middle life the bringing into an integrated whole of the dynamic, largely emotional, and often unconscious pattern by which the person relates to his society with the way in which we explain our behavior to ourselves and the acquired philosophy which we have taken in along the way.

Howe emphasizes the importance of coming to a genuine understanding of the significance of the personal in one's relationships with marriage partner, with teen-age children, and with God. The development of a faith for the middle years requires that one see personal relationships as more important than money, fame, things, pride, being right, or anything else.

We believe middle age has tremendous significance

religiously because of the maturity of mind and ability which is put into the service of God by laymen who see the burning bush or who hear the invitation of the Lord to give themselves completely in a ministry of whatever kind God may need. There is almost unlimited potential in what can happen if the power of God has its way in the abilities and resources of the middle aged. Here is one of the greatest challenges facing those of us engaged in Christian education.

LATER MATURITY

A. *Personality development*

We know so little of the great resources of ability and wisdom that exist in the years of later maturity because for the most part we have chosen in industry, commerce, and the church to retire persons from any opportunity to function in significant ways after they reach about sixty-five or seventy.

We do know that in later maturity some abilities wane while others reach their zenith. We know that there is much loneliness and a widespread feeling of no longer being of any worth. There is a great desire to be wanted and to have a feeling of being useful. There is much freedom to do creative work if one is invited to do it.

B. *Developmental tasks*

The tasks of later maturity are relatively few in number. There is the need (1) to adjust to decreasing strength and health, (2) to adjust to retirement and reduced income, (3) to adjust to the death of a companion, (4) to accept one's place among the elders of society, (5) to meet social and civic obligations, and (6) to establish living arrangements that are satisfactory.

C. Religious significance

People in later maturity are peculiarly open to the words of Jesus to Martha, "One thing is needful. . . ." These men and women are ready to simplify their lives —for their own sake and for God's sake. They are ready to slough off the less important things in order to give themselves to what is most important.

It is not accidental that a dear widowed lady who is eighty-two cherishes her Bible, her pastor, and her church as the most meaningful things left to her. It is not hard to understand that an eighty-year-old, almost-blind father spends large amounts of time listening to the reading of the Bible from his talking book machine. It is not hard to enlist older people in prayer circles, visiting teams, and all kinds of service projects.

There is little need for summary or conclusion. Each successive developmental period has its characteristics, its tasks, and its special openings for the God-man encounter. Perhaps the highest purpose of psychological data may be served when it provides the knowledge which makes more likely the bringing about of that encounter.

V

Toward a Theory of Christian Education

A major difference between the skilled practitioner in any field who is able to see his purposes fulfilled and the unskilled workman who constantly wonders why so little of what he hopes for comes to pass is that the skilled practitioner is theoretically oriented, designing operations to be consonant with the theory and modifying the theory from time to time as new data indicate the need. In nuclear physics and in man's adventurous probes into space it is the development of a body of theory that makes possible advances that read like science fiction. Theory provides a general framework within which many specific cases may be examined. A sound theory should provide a way to think about all cases which belong to a class. A sound theory should make possible the prediction of what the results will be given a certain pattern of situational factors.

More adequate work in Christian education requires the development of a body of theory about Christian education. We shall here want to draw together certain contributions from contemporary psychology that can contribute to developing a body of theory for Christian education. No pretense is made that what is said may be called a theory of Christian education. To do that requires one to draw not only on contemporary psychology and educational theory but also on what theology has to say about how God works with men, the difference between revelation and reason, the effect of sin in limiting what men can do, and the nature of the Church as the body within which persons are nurtured in faith. In this context only the former will be considered.

It will have become clear before this that as a psychologist who is also deeply involved in the Christian faith I have not hesitated to include men's encounter with God as valid data for psychological study and theorizing. In recent years my educational work and observation has been primarily with youth and with adults. The references, therefore, are almost entirely to the education of youth and adults. This is done without embarrassment, because the same principles that are to be found there are equally important in the education of children.

Our approach to a theory of Christian education is to look at a number of situations where the teaching-learning process was a lively one and then to see the importance of the maintenance of certain psychological tension systems in these teaching-learning situations. A general statement of the theory is that it is only as such tension systems are maintained that the teaching-learning process goes on. The examples are not limited to the teaching of Christian doctrine or values, for much theory that is relevant to any significant teaching is also relevant to the teaching of Christian doctrine and values. The choice is solely in terms of what seemed to be genuinely significant teaching-learning experiences.

SIGNIFICANT EXAMPLES OF TEACHING-LEARNING

It would be only the naïve theorist who today would claim that significant teaching and learning takes place only when one particular method or procedure is utilized. Because bad education is to be found in the use of a variety of methods and because significant teaching and learning can also be found in the use of the same methods, the examples chosen include quite different methods. The one thing they have in common is the fact that genuine education takes place in them all.

Example A

A church-school class of twelve high-school juniors and seniors with their teacher, a man who is also advisor to the youth program and with whom they work in many ways, are engaged in a study of the Gospel of Luke using only R.S.V. Bibles—and commentaries as they wish. The session is begun with a prayer that God may teach them the significance for their lives of the teaching of Jesus. One of the students reads aloud Luke 6:22-31. The teacher suggests that these seem like hard words and wonders aloud what they suggest to the members of the class. With some emotion a brilliant senior girl tells an event of the week that took place in the high-school orchestra where she plays violin. She and a boy from the class were objectors to war and to support of the

101

military establishment. The orchestra director made them stand before the remainder of the one-hundred members of the orchestra and said, "These two are the only ones who do not love their country enough to buy defense stamps." The other class members listened and asked questions. One said, "I believe that if we are faithful to Jesus' teaching there are times when we will be rejected and evil things will be said about us." There was a searching questioning among themselves as to whether popularity with the crowd should raise doubts about their Christian commitment. The period came to a close with no firm answers to questions but with the two feeling supported in what they had done for conscience' sake and with a greater readiness to doubt whether conformity with the other kids could be justified. They postponed until the next meeting discussion of how to act toward enemies. Obviously they wanted a full period for this.

Example B

The class is the first session of a course on "The Group in the Educational Process." The teacher is an internationally known psychoanalyst-educator. There are twelve students in the class. This first session is preceded by a great deal of tension and anxiety because the professor has a reputation that frightens students even at the graduate level. Chairs are arranged around a table. No one sits near the teacher on either side. The teacher begins with the question, "What is the meaning of the way we are sitting?" There is silence until finally one student ventures an answer. The teacher pounces on the answer and dissects it, forcing the person giving it to defend or to renounce it. So it is in every session. The content of the course is a tremendous, sometimes almost terrifying, always illuminating encounter between professor and student. Time after time the students are forced by the challenge of the teacher to keep asking themselves deeper and deeper questions about positions they have taken until their tension and anxiety make it intolerable any longer to give or support superficial answers to the most relevant questions of their relation to each other in the group. The most rigorous thinking, an openness to change of points of view, a new understanding of the educational process—these are what the student feels.

Example C

This teaching-learning experience is one of supervision of therapy of a thirteen-year-old boy by a practicing analytic therapist who is also a teacher. It is done in direct conversation between the supervisor and the therapist. On the preceding Monday evening the boy entered the office in friendly fashion and seemed to be continuing the good progress characteristic of several months of therapy. Half way through the hour he tentatively reached out and dug his fingernails into the therapist's hand. Within the next twenty minutes he kicked, hit, bit, and spit on the therapist and left the office much disturbed. The therapist was also disturbed. When he goes for his supervisory interview two days later he desperately needs to talk. He wants the supervisor to tell him the meaning of what has happened. The supervisor reassures him regarding the good work he has done with the boy and keeps the pressure on him to answer his own question. As he fumbles for explanation from the theoretical discussions of the class sessions, bits of insight begin to come. The supervisor accepts these bits of insights and presses with more questions. Additional insight comes slowly, corrected by challenges and questions when he starts in a wrong direction. Before the supervisory hour is over he has worked out his approach to the next hour of therapy on the basis of his new insights.

Example D

The experiences described here do not take place in a class situation at all. A counselor of a youth group is a topnotch basketball player and coaches the boys in the church league. After Friday-night practice and after the games the fellows gather with the counselor on the steps of the gym, around the kitchen table in the home of one of the boys, or at the drugstore. Often several of the girls from the youth group join them. The discussion usually starts with the game they have just played and their feelings about various things that happened. It never stops there. It covers the whole area of the concerns of teen-age youth. What standards should they hold to in their dating? What major should they take when they get to college? Shall they go into the armed services or into alternative service? What kind of abilities should a fellow have to consider the ministry as a vocation? What is the meaning of "being called by God"? If God is good, why does he permit an evil such as war to continue? What is likely to happen to a person after death? The young people ask the questions and share their ideas with each other. The counselor listens much, shares his own best insights, often cites what the Christian faith and ethic can contribute to thought on a particular question. These experiences are greatly valued by all the youth who participate.

Example E

The experience is two days in duration and designed to help the participants to come to some understanding of the forces that enter into the making of a decision that involves a whole community. It is preceded by a week of much less complex role-playing and lectures aimed at helping develop both empathy and intellectual insight for the individual functioning in a group. One person is in a role-play with one hundred others. He is chairman of a city-planning commission. He feels his inadequacy as he faces tasks that seem beyond him, as he answers questions for which there is insufficient data and insufficient time to gather accurate data. He faces the pressure to give information that is guess rather than fact. He sees the perpetual arguments between the French Canadian member of his staff and the conservative Midwesterner which prevent the accomplishment of anything significant toward the group task. He feels the pressures mount, his own defenses slip, and his patience wear thin. He sees other behavior in various groups in the played community just as irrational as his own. After the role-playing is over he hears a skilled political analyst put into clear perspective the forces which had been at work and build a clear statement of theory about community action.

Example F

Ninety students are in a systematic-theology class. The teacher comes in with several large volumes under his arm but with no notes. He introduces the topic for the next two or three days as the doctrine of the Trinity. He speaks of the radical positions which the early church attempted to avoid in their way of thinking of the nature of God. The picture of dualism as it was to be found in Marcion or in Arius and of Monism as found in pantheism or Monarchianism becomes vivid before the students. He shows the concern of the church to give devotion to the God of the Old Testament, their conviction that salvation is in Christ, but that since salvation can be only in God their emergent binitarianism. Tertullian comes alive as he becomes a protagonist for the Holy Spirit. The teacher shows the contribution of Basil, Gregory, and Augustine to the development. He relates the development of the doctrine to the kind of thinking that had been characteristic of the Greek philosophers. He

106

evaluates Barth's position on the Trinity. He gives a clear statement of his own position. Several times he picks up one of the large volumes and translates from the Latin as he reads an excerpt to the class. What does the student do? He takes notes, and he finds himself thinking forward and backward from where the teacher is at the moment, probing, relating, questioning, integrating. It is an hour of furious intellectual activity which is intimately related to many of the problems with which the student has struggled.

These experiences have been chosen and described because they are illustrative of the great experiences through which a person's insights are kindled, questions answered, knowledge integrated, and behavior modified. After each of these one had the feeling that in a sense he was a "new person." It is not for a moment meant to imply that in any of these there is any substitute for what happens when a man encounters God in Christ and a "new creature" comes into being. It is suggested that, built on the experience of being made new by the God-man encounter, there may be many experiences of an educative kind in which significant changes take place in the person.

What does a psychologist see in such experiences that may be useful for the Christian educator? Let it be said that he sees no clear and easy direction in which if a teacher goes he will certainly be a good teacher. It is more likely that the characteristics of significant teaching-learning are always themselves in the form of tension between this and that. In the remainder of this presentation an attempt will be made to identify six such tension systems that characterize the most fruitful teaching-learning process and go a long way toward a theory of Christian education.

TENSION SYSTEMS IN PRODUCTIVE TEACHING-LEARNING

By tension systems we mean seeming bipolarities that characterize the good teaching-learning situation in such manner that neither pole may be ignored without severe injury to the process. Let us look at these bipolarities to see how they are characteristic of teaching at every age level and of profound importance if effective Christian education is to take place.

A. *There is tension between the "single one"-ness of the teacher and the threat that he feels when he enters into communication with students*

Great teaching takes place only when the teacher has as a "single one," alone, an authentic person, stood before reality and come to know himself in relation to that reality. He must become a real person before he can help to call others into genuine personhood. Being someone can continue only as the teacher continues to deal with reality. If he dodges the hard reality of contemporary life by flight into words or ideas that do not adequately represent that reality or by doling out the shadows of an experience of reality of twenty years ago or twenty-hundred years ago he will be unable to evoke true personhood in others or to lead them into richer insights and relation-ships—i.e., he will be unable to participate in their education.

The core of authenticity which is the teacher can never evoke growth and change in the student, however, unless there is encounter, dialogue, conversation, or communication. So the teacher has the responsibility to give up to some degree his singleness, his privacy, his aloneness in order to communicate with the student. Whenever there is genuine encounter and communication something of the teacher is given. There is the possibility, indeed the necessity, of challenge if the student is to be anything more than a parrot imitating what his master says or a cormorant regurgitating the fish for the master fisherman.

The good teacher does not develop conversation or dialogue between the student and himself only, but between the student and the great thinkers of the past, or between the student and the voices of contemporary culture. In Example F the student felt during the lecture that he was in conversation with Tertullian, Eusebius, Basil, Augustine—that he was involved in the council where the creed was hammered out. Because there were ninety to one hundred pupils this was primarily a mental process induced by the lecturer, but it was nonetheless encounter and dialogue with the great. In Examples B, C, and D there was constant dialogue and challenge. This was the essence of the teaching-learning process—and let it be clear that it is both teacher and student who are

109

learning in the dialogue. Nathaniel Cantor not only did this kind of teaching beautifully, but summed it up when he said, "One of the important characteristics of skilled teaching is the creation of an atmosphere which encourages pupils to question, challenge, and contribute to one another's and to the teacher's growth." [1] At another point he indicated one of the real values of this kind of experience for the pupil: "When the instructor accepts challenge and criticism it becomes easy for students to admit weakness." [2]

It would be a mistake to see dialogue and encounter as a kind of educational or teaching technique or gadget. Rather it is to be seen as the very core of the teaching process. Ross Snyder expressed this idea most adequately when he said:

We have sometimes failed to see that intellectual encounter (even combat) is a necessary form of group process —(it is a way we bind ourselves into "a people"); and we get acquainted with the core of each other in matching ourselves against the life and death issues of our time. And so this is a mutual ministry, not an academic gadget. [3]

We should not underestimate the costliness and pain of this part of teaching—especially for the beginning teacher, but in a very real sense for all of us. It is so much more comfortable, there is so much less risk if the teacher

[1] *The Teaching-Learning Process* (New York: The Dryden Press, 1953), pp. 79-80.

[2] *Ibid.*, pp. 86-87.

[3] *Creative Teaching Concerning the Church in Student-Professor Relationships* (Mimeographed document), p. 34.

will wrap himself in an academic title, ensconce himself behind the bulwark of a lecture desk—even better if it is elevated somewhat in order to heighten the distance between teacher and student, protect his vulnerable areas by preparation of a lecture that will last from the opening bell to the closing one, and have a committee meeting awaiting him immediately following the class period. Of course, the same kind of defenses can be described which the teacher may use in various other teaching methods. A man takes a risk, makes himself vulnerable, when he conceives of the need for dialogue in teaching. There is a threat to him as a person, but if teaching is to be exciting for both student and teacher this is a tension system that must exist.

B. *There is tension between the "Thus saith the Lord"-ness of the Bible and the necessity of translating the myth of a day that is past save in poetic discourse into the thought forms of contemporary life*

A distinctive characteristic of Christian education will always be its dependence for a word from God himself upon the Scriptures. The teacher in the church believes that not only did the prophets find it possible and proper to proclaim "Thus saith the Lord your God," but also that there is a deeper sense in which it can be said of the Scriptures from the beginning to the end—"Thus saith the Lord." In Example A the young people found themselves again and again returning to the idea that

God himself says to his people, "Woe unto you when all speak well of you." The church-school teacher will hear God speak a word most profoundly in Jesus Christ but with eyes of faith will hear God speak long before through his servant Israel. The sophisticated teacher will not be too ready to eliminate large sections of the Scriptures for teaching youth or children because they describe people as they were—and are. He will realize that the stories are no more lurid than the ones the child reads or sees every day and that they are told in the perspective of a God who watches to judge, chasten, and redeem.

This perception of the Bible must be held in tension with the idea which Rudolf Bultmann has helped to dramatize for us all. The concepts of the Bible in many cases are not those with which contemporary man thinks. We face the constant necessity, therefore, while giving up not one jot or tittle of the truth that God speaks, to translate that truth into the myth and the language of the twentieth century. We no longer live in a "three-storied universe," but men still live so as to cut themselves off completely from God or so live in faith that they need to go up no stairs to find heaven. For the Christian teacher it is the difficult but imperative task to hold these two poles in tension—never to lose the authentic Word of God and always to translate it into the language of the twentieth century.

C. *There is tension between the need for movement through and coverage of material and provision for the immediate needs of the students*

112

No matter what material a church-school teacher may teach, he always faces the problem of covering some reasonable amount in the time which is available. We set certain goals for ourselves in terms of the things we think children should know about Christian faith by the completion of a certain grade. Almost everyone agrees that for a person to be an intelligent, functioning Christian there are certain things he should know. These a teacher is responsible, therefore, to teach.

Because of recognition of such needs curriculum committees build a curriculum. For the same reason the competent teacher establishes the goals of a course and either on paper or in his mind works out a schedule for the movement from where the students are now to where the school wants them to be as a result of this course. To use a term from social psychology, this is the "task orientation" of the teacher and is related to the goals of the particular curriculum and course of study. But as a class of twenty-five is exposed to a body of knowledge individuals will have questions, needs for clarification of issues, needs to challenge a point of view because it does violence to their present view. It is at this point that the tension arises between the "task orientation" of the teacher and the needs of the individual and group.

The tension does not exist just between professor and class, but also between an orientation toward locomotion and an orientation toward concern for the immediate needs of pupils. If true education is to take place there must be some recognition of these immediate needs. The problem is to hold some balance between "getting on with" the material and treating students as persons. Some students in any class are often more rigorously task oriented than the teacher. The teacher out of his experience may realize the inevitability of the tension; these students say, "Rule out the questions and discussion and get on with the lecture." There are other students who frankly admit to the release of many a hare simply to draw the fox off the trail which might lead to a revelation of their own inadequacy on that particular day.

Social psychology has shown quite conclusively that work groups get the most work done and get it done most happily when there is a happy balance between task orientation and what is called individual and group maintenance. This then seems to be one of the tension systems that the teacher will experience if he does good teaching.

D. *There is tension between the need for experiencing and for conceptualizing, between practice and theory*

It has often been said that we learn by doing, but for the varied tasks of the Christian in the world this is not an adequate kind of learning. Certain kinds of skills can be learned by just doing an act over and over, increasing its perfection. However, it is as the act of ministering is conceptualized that it becomes for the Christian more than a skill—it becomes a ministry.

For conceptualizing, theorizing, or theologizing to be

fruitful it must be based on experience by the student. In Example F the professor by his skill provides an internal experience rich in images as he pictures the conflicts and needs out of which the doctrine of the Trinity emerged. In Example E the trainers provided an experience one step closer to the real thing. The role-playing gave the student many of the same feelings and perceptions he might have had in a real-life community issue and capped it with a theory session. In Example A a vivid description helps all to experience encounter. In Example B the experience of the class encounter itself is the content of the course which the student puts together conceptually. In Example C the experience comes in therapy of the boy, is brought to the supervisory interview, is conceptualized, and future experience is planned in the light of the theory.

In a time when the need is so great for Christian lay ministries with a strong inner core of authenticity there is little use for people who have a repertoire of tricks and plays that they can use like trained seals. Nor is there much use for people who have all the proper concepts suitably expressed in correct words but with no experience of the reality out of which the concepts emerged.

We are responsible as Christian educators to so plan that students shall go out of our schools prepared for a ministry of Christian laity by having been through the tension of experience giving birth to concepts and practice to theory under the midwifery of the teachers.

115

E. *There is tension between the full recognition by the teacher that he cannot lead God to where a man waits and the teacher's awareness of the critical importance of the student's encounter with the Almighty*

The Christian teacher knows both from his understanding of the nature of God and from his own observation of God's work that his arm cannot be twisted to make him walk in a certain place at a certain time. God is not to be domesticated and led around at the desire of even the most devout of his children. The teacher knows it is not possible and more, that if it were possible, that would be the death of God as God.

Yet the deepest desire of many a Christian teacher is that a teen-age boy or girl, a middle-aged man or woman, may see the burning bush, may hear the voice, may meet the Lord God. He wishes for this because he knows that in this kind of encounter life is changed radically.

What then is the answer? If the teacher may not venture to take the hand of God and lead him where he may meet the lost one, then at least he may take the arm of the lost one and lead him to walk in a place where God may be met. This is what may be seen in Example D. These young people in some cases met God while they talked about eternal matters around a kitchen table or on the steps of a gymnasium. If education is Christian education this tension must always exist.

F. *There is forever the tension between the need to establish an emotional climate in which it is safe to try to create and try out new modes of behavior and to maintain the kind of anxiety in the student without which no fundamental change can take place*

The creation of a climate in which it is safe to present an idea just born for the consideration of teacher and one's peers is probably necessary for any development of creativity, and especially necessary for the student whose ego structure is not tough but somewhat fragile. It is probably clear to all of us what happens to a four-year-old who runs to show her daddy a picture she has just drawn of their home and family only to be met with the words, "But Mary, who ever saw a green dog, and our house has one story instead of two, and Daddy is really taller than Mother. I'd do it this way." Is it equally clear what happens to young theological students in their first efforts at preaching when the professor publicly or privately says, "But John, the text could not possibly mean what you have suggested. There ought to be two major divisions in your sermon instead of three. Now, if I were doing it, I would do it this way."? Have we asked ourselves what happens to the ego structure of the student who has an insight as to the meaning of a sequence of events in church history but is met with hoots of laughter from the teacher who has himself devised the correct interpretation of this same series of events?

We may well ask ourselves how it is possible to provide in the teaching-learning situations of a church school the same kind of security for trial of the new idea or the new mode of behavior that the good parent or kindergarten teacher knows is a necessity for establishing the roots of creativity in a child. If we do not ask ourselves the question and struggle through to a satisfactory answer shall we be surprised if the members of our churches are "organization men," conformists, and "other directed"? One of the really difficult issues here is the tension between freedom to inquire, to research, perhaps to give birth to new interpretations, and the necessity to follow the confessional position. Surely here there are no easy answers, and this is one of the major issues with which the teacher must struggle if he looks at the problem theologically.

The other pole of this tension system is the necessity to create, clarify, or maintain some kind of anxiety in the student which will motivate change. This issue had never become clear for me until I had the experiences of Examples B and E. Things were learned about organizational life in a community and about relationships to other people in a situation in Example E where, under very heavy pressures, one had to learn. In Example B the class was approached with a great buildup of anxiety. The anxiety decreased from class to class but there was always high tension. Learning and change came in ways that will never be forgotten. As the importance of this element in the teaching-learning situation became clearer my own classes probably were not as pleasant for the students but more growth and learning took place.

Then some of what had been read began to have significance.

Harry Stack Sullivan, a great and original thinker in the sciences of man, declared that the very worst method of educating children is to create anxiety in them. The second worst method, he added, is not to generate any anxiety in them. Cantor said, "Indeed, from a mental-hygiene point of view, the function of responsible adults —parents and teachers—is to provide sufficient guilt and anxiety to stimulate the acceptance of personal and social obligations." [4] Martin Buber spoke, I think, of the same necessity when he said, "To keep the pain awake, to waken the desire—that is the first task of everyone who regrets the obscuring of eternity. It is also the first task of the genuine educator in our time." [5] Although Sullivan backs away from the creation of too great anxiety in children, all these writers say that education takes place only where there is anxiety and pain sufficient to motivate change. This is the second pole of the tension system.

One is certainly tempted to ask how these two poles can possibly be maintained in the same system. No easy way can be suggested. Surely it cannot be done if one has the romantic idea that love and security are all that is needed for development of the person. It requires the understanding that movement toward maturity comes through the experience of pain and anxiety as well as

[4] *Op. cit.,* p. 31.

[5] Martin Buber, *Between Man and Man,* trans. by Ronald G. Smith (New York: Macmillan, 1947), p. 111.

love and security. The teacher in Example B puts this in the title of one of his books, *Love Is Not Enough*.[6]

I am aware of the gaps in this attempt at the psychological aspects of a theory of Christian education. Certainly we have not said, "Use this technique of teaching and you will be a good Christian educator." What has been proposed is that excellent Christian teaching, no matter what the method, contains these tension systems. The examples contain varying balances within these tension systems. Good teaching has learned to fear none of the poles in the tension systems and uses the poles boldly, all the while maintaining a balance between them that helps the students move toward true Christian maturity.

---

[6] Bruno Bettelheim (Chicago: Free Press, 1950).

INDEX

PSYCHOLOGY
and the
Teaching Church

JESSE H. ZIEGLER

Two major areas of knowledge are necessary for the effective Christian teacher. First, he must know God personally and intimately. Next, he must know man. One means of accomplishing the latter is "by way of the kind of empirical and systematic study that is characteristic of contemporary psychology." It is on this approach that this book is concentrated.

From the science of psychology Dr. Ziegler surveys and interprets that which is most relevant and important for Christian education. He proceeds by reviewing the main trends in psychological theory about personality and progresses to the learning theory, developmental characteristics, group process, and educational theory.

In presenting examples of tested teaching-learning "psychological tension systems," Dr. Ziegler makes a significant contribution that will be of

(continued on the back flap)